SWIMMING UPSTREAM

A FISH BIOLOGIST'S JOURNEY

DAVID LEVY

ISBN 979-8-31781-245-4 eBook 979-8-31781-246-1

"Many men go fishing all of their lives without knowing that it is not fish they are after."

— *Henry David Thoreau*

"Fishing is an affirmation of life's richness and our profound interconnecteness to the natural world."

— *Carl Safina*

"Fishing provides the opportunity of being totally immersed, turning back into yourself in a good way."

— *Ted Hughes*

"Why do I like fishing? Its all about the journey and any catch is a bonus. The best part is going down to the boat in the early morning, smelling the boat exhaust and the salty sea air, watching the sunrise, and hanging with your fishing buddies."

— *Dave Levy*

Contents

A LIFETIME OF FISHING

I remember fishing with my Dad on the St. Lawrence River for pike, perch and bass and trolling for blue-fish off Massachusetts which were good fighters and good eaters. We also went ice fishing on Lake Memphremagog east of Montreal although the details are sketchy. The photo shows me in the yellow toque, a lifelong friend, Barry Krumholtz in the brown Baklava and my brother Bob. The latter two had highly successful careers as physicians while I pursued a lifetime of fishing.

These early experiences ignited my interest in anything that swam. The first serious fishing I undertook targeted salmon in the Salish Sea adjacent to Vancouver. Initially the pickings were slim, but over time and with the advice of friends, I learned how to catch salmon. I pursued fishing strategies described in a book by Charles White called: "How to Catch Salmon: Advanced Techniques ."

Fast forward 20 years when I began working at the University of British Columbia and encountered Europeans and Asians who were fishing for surf smelt on evening flood tides. I obtained smelt nets and chest waders and determined that the most productive fishing area was Wreck Beach.

We set our nets perpendicular to shore and lit a bonfire. Often, a couple of hours would elapse with nothing, then all hell would break loose, and you would have a netful of wriggling smelt. At the end of the evening, after the tide had turned, we would regroup at someone's apartment for a smelt fry and complete annihilation of the host's kitchen.

The Latin name for surf smelt is *Hypomesus pretiosus* and the word *pretiosus* means "precious", in reference to their delicious flavour. We cooked them like small trout after they were cleaned, dipped in egg and flour, fried up in a hot pan, and drizzled with lemon juice. Smelt fishing was low tech, required minimal fishing skills, cost next to nothing, was a social affair and provided some of the best fishing that I ever experienced.

I became interested in the biology of surf smelt and determined there was little scientific information. I waded in and embarked on a surf smelt study at Wreck Beach, assisted by four enthusiastic summer students. Wreck Beach is famous since it is a nude beach, but that was a distraction for our research. One of the students owned a large German Shepherd which she brought to our sampling site and that was the end of any unwanted harassment.

Biology and Management of Surf Smelt in Burrard Inlet, Vancouver, B.C.

David A. Levy

Westwater Research Centre
Technical Report No. 28

My fishing opportunities expanded when my wife Karen and I purchased a 24-foot sailboat that we christened "Sludge" in view of her humble beginnings (see Crusin'). We cruised up to Pender Harbour and caught coho under sail, a challenging and satisfying feat. One day there was a pack of boats anchored beside Thormanby Island mooching live herring. We trolled through the middle of the pack and picked up a chunky spring (Chinook) salmon then sailed on towards Vancouver. The surrounding fishing boats cheered us on.

We had a family friend from Montreal, Mickey Gold, who was very keen on salmon fishing. His daughter Harriet had moved to Vancouver, married, and produced 2 boys, one of whom is my godson, and the other is Karen's godson. This provided Mickey with ample excuses to visit Vancouver, and every time he showed up, he and I made our way to Campbell River and fished with a professional guide and good friend, Mike Barker, out of a 15-foot Boston Whaler with tiller steering. One of Mickey's trademarks was an uncanny ability to tell jokes. Due to the internet, joke telling has become a lost art and Mickey perfected timing, accents, cadence and follow-ups that would keep Mike and I in stitches.

My two closest fishing buddies are Itsuo Yesaki (aka Its) and Hermann Enzenhofer. Hermann and Its fish steelhead in the Vedder River and both are ace fishermen. In Hermann's case he always catches the first fish, the heaviest fish, the most fish and the bragging rights that go with.

We previously worked together in the Fraser River conducting SONAR surveys and shared a passion for fishing. We were keen to try fishing in Haida Gwaii and investigated the numerous high-end fishing lodges that provide some of the best salmon fishing on the planet. I called up Herman and Its. "Sorry to tell you this guys, we are going to need second mortgages to afford a fishing trip to Haida Gwaii".

We let it sit for a while, then Hermann called up excitedly one day, saying he had located a reasonably priced outfit in Masset called "Jerry's Fishing Charters". Jerry was a semi-trailer driver from Alberta and had purchased several apartments that were formerly owned by the Canadian military. We signed up and flew to Masset. Jerry turned out to be an intolerant red neck with lots of rough edges and prejudices. He was nasty towards his clients, but they nevertheless put up with his unfriendly behaviour because the salmon fishing was so good.

There were more customers than boat places, so Jerry called for backup, and we were introduced to Peewee who is Haida and has spent most of his life fishing for spring salmon close to Masset. Peewee showed up with a 25-foot welded aluminum fishing boat with twin Yamaha outboards. Immediately there was good energy on board, and we ended up returning to Masset for many years and always fished with Peewee. Peewee never used a fishing net and relied on his commercial fishing skills to gaff any fish into the boat. I would watch and cringe, lest he knock the hook out of the fishes' mouth. However, that never happened.

Peewee was an artist and assisted Reg Davidson, a famous Haida carver. Peewee introduced us to Reg who explained his craft. The totem pole that Reg was working on during our visit now stands in Vancouver Airport. "The Raven with a Broken Beak" is inspired by a Haida legend in which Raven attempts to play a joke on a blind fisherman. Raven dove into the sea to steal the bait from the man's halibut hook. The old man's fishing line caught Raven's beak and quickly broke it off. Unsure of what had happened to his hook, the blind man asked his daughter to put the bill on a stick and raise it up above his house. An ashamed Raven emerged from the sea and tried to reattach the beak to his face, but it slipped and instead became attached to his chin, causing even more shame.

We enjoyed great fishing in Haida Gwaii and would fish hard for 3.5 days, fly back to Vancouver, and then want to go fishing again the next day. This is not unlike other addictions that can take over your life.

The holy grail of salmon fishing is catching a Tyee: a spring salmon over 30 pounds. Hermann caught one on our first visit that took a few runs before flipping onto a kelp bed making the fish easy to retrieve. Its hooked one and had it on the line for about 20 mins before it broke off. This induced a severe black funk that settled over the boat.

In 2011 we returned to Haida Gwaii brimming with anticipation. We started by trolling through a heavy downpour before the clouds parted and the sun poked out. It was flat calm, an unusual sea state for Haida Gwaii. Peewee suggested removing our flashers and fishing the lines with medium-sized spoons. This setup had the advantage that if you hooked something, it would only be you and the fish, with no interference from a flasher.

When the salmon hit, the rod pointed down vertically as the downrigger released. I knew right away that it was a Tyee.

There were no boats around us so Peewee switched off the engines and it was just me and the salmon for around 40 minutes. The reel screamed multiple times when the salmon ran. I screened out of all the coaching, words of encouragement, swearing, sarcastic remarks and joking and focussed on getting the fish into the boat. Peewee gaffed the spring, and a round of high fives ensued. The fish of a lifetime.

We would regularly jig for halibut with good success off Tow Hill near a large sand flat where halibut would sit on the bottom feeding on herring and juvenile crabs. These were "chicken halibut", relatively easy to catch and perfect for eating.

We had been successful for salmon fishing and each of us had two Styrofoam coolers of frozen, vacuum sealed portions of prime Haida Gwaii spring and coho salmon. We were on our final outing and planned to fly out from Masset Airport later that afternoon. Around 11:30, Hermann's rod bent over and he hooked a lunker. There was no way he could control the fish. We speculated about what kind of fish it was. A shark? A side-saddled huge salmon?

After around 45 minutes the fish came up from the depths and we could see a massive halibut. It took all four of us to bring it in using a welded rebar hook and myself securing Peewee so he could lean over the side. After we strongarmed the fish into the boat, it flopped around violently so Peewee hog tied it, and we ran back to port.

We stopped at the commercial landing station and the fish weighed in at 164 lb. Peewee filleted 120 pounds of meat. Now what? We didn't have capacity to transport any fish when Peewee proposed a solution. In Masset, if you donate your fish, the processor will donate vacuum sealing, and the fish would be provided to patients in Masset Hospital. A win-win solution. I kept a large chunk and brought it to a St'át'imc feast in the Interior. The halibut was the first food item consumed and my St'át'imc friends raved about it.

A couple of years later a friend, Don MacDonald who lives in Nanaimo, invited Karen and I to spend a weekend fishing at Ucluelet on Vancouver Island.

We had considerable success on a Friday evening and caught our limit of springs. The next day the rain pelted down and the wind was howling so Karen and I opted out and brought out the Scrabble Board. The rest of the crew including two boys, poked around a sheltered bay having a nice, miserable time catching rockfish. They came back looking like drowned rats and parked themselves beside the fireplace. We woke up early on Sunday and the wind was still howling and the rain was still pelting down. We decided that we would abort the effort and come back another day. The first order of business was to retrieve the boat and load it onto the trailer. There were a few challenges: the tide was out, the boat was heavy, and the launch ramp was steep and slippery.

To get the boat onto the trailer, Don backed the trailer down to the edge of the boat ramp and I muscled/winched the boat until it was properly seated on the trailer. We then jockeyed the boat, trailer and truck and picked up maybe 12 inches of cable before the winch froze due to the heavy load. Don surveyed the situation and announced: "Out of the way!". He then cranked the winch hard, freeing the ratchet and the handle started to helicopter wildly.

Unfortunately, Don's hand was in the way, and the handle struck his middle finger, exposing around 2 inches of bone at an oblique angle to his hand.

I was shocked and my heart was pounding. I told myself this is no time to panic, get some help and get Don to a First Aid Clinic. I called Mary Lou, Don's partner, and she drove Don to Tofino for first aid, and from there, to Nanaimo General Hospital where they operated on Don's hand around midnight.

Karen and I looked after the 2 boys, consulted the tide tables to determine the timing of high tide, hooked up the boat to the trailer, drove to Nanaimo, dropped off the truck and boat, then headed for BC Ferries.

What is the moral of this story? Accidents can happen anytime on boats, some are benign, some can injure and some can be lethal, especially if male egos are involved. It is advantageous and highly desirable to retain a vigilant attitude of "boat sense" to avoid preventable boating accidents. Our Ucluelet accident could have been avoided entirely just by waiting for the high tide.

Mike Barker, who guided us 30 years previously in Campbell River, contacted me via LinkedIn to ask if I'd be interested in a "deeply discounted" fishing trip to Kyuquot Sound. Over 30 years, he and I had gone our separate ways, had families, careers, joys, and sadnesses while I pursued consulting and Mike pursued his guiding business. Over time, fishing in Campbell River slowed down. Mike adjusted by establishing a small fishing lodge and guiding business, Kyuquot Beach House, on Northwest Vancouver Island. To make the business work, he needed to fill up his boats. There was a party of lawyers from LA, and they needed an eighth person. It didn't take a lot of convincing, and I joined the group, sharing with them my best lawyer jokes.

Since that trip we have gone to Kyuquot numerous times and have enjoyed spectacular fishing and west coast scenery.

FISH TANK

LEVY BOYS

STURGEON FISHING

Sport fishing took a dive during COVID and a few of the lodges, particularly those which relied upon American customers, were hurting. Several outfits were offering deep discounts that were too good to pass up. We ended up visiting Nootka Island Resort several times and enjoyed good salmon and halibut fishing.

Hermann and I decided to run offshore one day for some halibut fishing. It was calm with few waves, making for good jigging conditions. Shortly after we dropped our lines, Hermann' s rod started to shake. There is some skill required to hook halibut, and it is best to wait 20-30 seconds before setting the hook. Then a tug of war starts and when close to the boat, the fish needs to be carefully measured prior to gaffing. Hermann played it perfectly and was rewarded with a 40 lb halibut, one of the best forms of protein on the planet.

We dropped our lines again and the bite slowed down. We were enjoying the fishing vibe while our guide Shane was trying to unravel a tangled halibut reel. Suddenly he slipped and the entire rig went overboard. This is not a good way to operate, and Shane was choked as the rod and reel belonged to a fellow guide and he had his reputation to think about. Suddenly, my rod tip started to shake and I hooked a halibut.

As the fish was coming in the line went slack. Damn, the fish was off. I kept reeling but there was no fish. I reeled some more and saw that one of the bare hooks had snagged a fishing line.

My explanation for these observations is as follows: Shane's line had gone down and there was line paid out close to the bottom. I then hooked a halibut which swam beside the line while I reeled in. The fish got off and the line was hooked and retrieved by my rod. I admit there are other hypotheses. Shane was ecstatic about retrieving his gear and washed off the reel in freshwater, concluding that his halibut rig was supercharged and would fearlessly catch halibut in future.

It was exciting to see the marine life. While fishing in Haida Gwaii, Kyuquot, Nootka Sound and Knight Inlet we saw orcas, humpback whales, dolphins, sea otters, ocean sunfish and seabirds.

Prawning and Crabbing in Knight Inlet

Mike Barker wanted to expand his business to include prawn fishing experiences in Knight Inlet which he test drove by inviting some fishing buddies who had previously been up to Kyuquot. Base camp was a precariously leaning float home with algae-covered floorboards. We used a "prawn puller" to help retrieve our traps set in 200 – 250 feet of water. Without a doubt, spot prawns are the best tasting prawns in the North Pacific and prawning in Knight Inlet has been productive.

We also set crab traps. After we first arrived, Mike pulled up a submerged blue tank containing around 15 legal-sized Dungeness crabs. While we were at base camp, we consumed quite a few. However, we constantly had crab pots fishing and would introduce the freshly caught crab into the blue tank. We therefore created a sustainable crab fishery, and crab became a staple food item. We tried out numerous prawn and crab recipes. One of the crew, Doug Anzai from Quadra Island, is a superb seafood chef who likes to experiment

Mexico

Over the years I have gone deep-sea fishing in Acapulco, Cabo San Lucas and Zihuatanejo.

Acapulco

I described our fishing experiences in Acapulco in a December 1998 Christmas letter to friends and business associates.

In December, 1998 the Levy family flew to Acapulco for a mid-winter break. Following a Mexican breakfast, it was time to hit the pool at the "La Palapa Hotel" located on the shore of Acapulco Bay. Within 5 minutes we were approached by Angelo, the local water sports agent who lines up SCUBA diving, jet-skiing, parasailing, banana-boating, and deep-sea fishing. My ears perked up when he mentioned fishing,

Angelo asked if I wanted to see the pictures. Sure enough, there were large fish to be had although the charter prices for the miniature Queen Mary's (many thousands per day) seemed a little prohibitive. In my best Spanish, I asked Angelo if perhaps there were some less expensive boats available, and we eventually settled on the Z Mares III, chartering out at $200 per day.

The next morning, Angelo took us down to the fishing pier to meet Jésus, el Capitan, and Oscar, the first mate. We set out as the sun rose over Acapulco Bay filled with optimism for a fish. As we headed offshore, Oscar sewed large hooks into the baitfish (mullets). Oscar and Jésus set-out the two outriggers and we trolled rapidly with 4 @ 200 pound test lines attached to the outriggers and 3 lines dead astern (the first baited with a large vicious-looking squid lure, the second with a bonito flopping on the surface, and a third line with plastic squids (teaser lines) which served as attractors for the other bait lines). It was calm with a rolling swell. Two hours passed and we slathered on #30 SBF suntan lotion. The boys were getting cranky.

Oscar is on the flying bridge driving the boat, while Jésus is tending the lines keeping us entertained with Mexican fish stories. Jésus looks at the inside outrigger line with a peculiar expression. He grabs the rod, and yards back vigorously. "Martin, marlin, marlin"! he yells, and next thing, a massive black marlin breaks the surface and is tail walking, 50 m behind the boat. Jésus is sending out a staccato, machine-gun fire stream of Spanish invectives, understandable only to Mexicans. Up walking on his tail comes the marlin again, for a third time, a fourth time, and a fifth time!

The marlin disappears. Suddenly, the reel starts to scream! The marlin has taken off and Jésus runs up to the bow of the boat, yelling at Oscar to chase the fish. The marlin comes up again for the sixth time, only now, he is 50 m in front of the boat, moving like a bloody locomotive!

Dave comes to his senses and begins to haul in the other lines and clear the deck. We are in for a scrap. Jésus passes over the rod and instructs me to take a seat in the fishing chair and gives me the 30-second accelerated instructional course on marlin fishing. The principles involve:

1. *Keep modest tension on the line at all times;*
2. *If the fish tail walks, reel like hell;*
3. *Yard back on the rod slowly with clutch engaged; and*
4. *Reel in as much line as possible on the down stroke.*

Thirty minutes go by, 45 minutes and then an hour. I am drenched in sweat and getting seriously tired! Jésus takes over so I can take a 10-minute break and then I'm "back in the saddle". I learn the 2-handed version of the upstroke, which makes life somewhat easier. With an arduous effort on my part for 15 minutes, I take in about 30 m of line. The marlin makes a run and undoes my hard effort in about 30 seconds!

Am I giving up? Never!

After ninety minutes we notice a change in the angle of the line. The marlin is sounding and is now 30 m below the boat. It feels like we have caught the mother of all halibuts. Whereas before, there was some give-and-take between the marlin and me, now we are at a stalemate. We innovate. Jésus puts the rod tip over his shoulder and very slowly hand lines the marlin while I take up the slack on the reel. The plan is to get the marlin close to the boat where we will either hook him with a second rod or else sink in a vicious looking grapple hook tied to a nylon rope. We are getting a little bit frustrated. Jésus has an idea. We'll crank up the tension on

my rod and clip it to rod #2 which has a much stronger reel. Jésus clips rod #1 on #2 and drops rod #1 into the water. Next thing, rod #1 is swimming away from us and the line from rod #2 is fluttering in the breeze.

Captain Antonio Romero with a 362 lb black marlin from Cabo San Lucas, Baja California Sur.

I look up in stunned disbelief. Jésus has taken the rod with a huge marlin attached and HE HAS THROWN IT AWAY! Of all the stupid, imbecilic things I have ever witnessed, this one is the ultimate! Jésus is looking out over the water, on the verge of tears, absolutely dumbfounded.

I recover. "Jésus don't worry about the fish, it's not that important" (thinking, Mexicans have been separated from their cojones for actions much less serious than this!). "After all. I am fortunate to have had the experience of playing a big marlin for 2 hours" (thinking, you will be hearing from my attorney, and I will be taking an action against you!). "It's early, we can still fish some more" (thinking, I now understand why Hemingway committed suicide — he was playing a marlin off Havana for 2 hours and dropped his rod overboard!).

Jésus goes up to the flying bridge to drive, while Oscar sets out the lines again. I notice that Oscar is trying to stay as far away from Jésus as possible. We troll. A pall of depression settles over the boat. I climb up to the flying bridge with 2 Coronas for a heart-to-heart with Jésus. Jésus too, is not all that worried about the fish — he's worried about the $US 250 Penn reel and his reputation as a fishing guide. We find an acceptable solution. I will make a cash contribution towards a new deep-sea fishing rig, and (within Mexico) will keep a lid on the story about how we came to lose the fish. We shake hands. Life can resume.

Following our return to port, fried to a crisp, we flop into the hotel pool. Angelo comes over for a full debriefing. He then runs over to some freshly arrived gringos, announcing to all within earshot: "the guy over there caught a huge marlin today!" I am beginning to think that Angelo has an MBA in marketing from Harvard Business School.

Two days later, we again head out on a sister boat to the Z Mares Ill called "Jésus Boat" and meet Capitan Chucho, Mario the first mate, and Armando the second mate. We set out the lines and head offshore, beyond site of land. There are light winds and a rolling sea. "Look over there, the fin of a sailfish!" "Over there, 2 sailfish!" "Another one over there!". The place was fishy.

We are sitting on the flying bridge talking with Chucho while the first and second mates do their thing. Suddenly, Mario grabs a rod and sets the hook into a sailfish. We have one! The line goes peeling out. I take my place in the fishing chair and start the classical deep-sea up-and-down fishing and reeling pattern. He's a serious contender but a lightweight compared to the marlin. Armando asks if I would like a beer while I am fighting the fish, thereby rounding out the deep-sea fishing experience. I decline. Within 15 minutes, the fish is beside the boat.

We set out the lines again and troll around. Chucho, who has a sixth sense about fish, jumps down from the flying bridge and grabs the middle rod with the squid lure. A sailfish is following it. He pays out some slack and tries to entice a strike. The fish appears to have moved on.

Suddenly, Mario spots him again, this time following the bait on one of the outrigger lines. He grabs the rod, flicks it out of the outrigger quick-release, and rapidly spools out line from the reel. After ten seconds he throws the switch on the reel, waits for the tension on the line to build, presses his thumb against the spool and pulls back on the rod to set the hook.

"We've got him! Mario you beautiful man!".

I ran into Jésus at the pier from the first outing and he firmly believes that I am a lucky asset on board and vows to get me another marlin.

I booked the Z Mares III for a final day on the water. I arrive at the fishing pier at 07:00 and am greeted by Jésus. Where is Oscar the first mate? According to some local fishermen, *he was seen the previous night drinking tequila with his brothers. We begin a search for Oscar.*

The sun is coming up, all the fishing boats have left port, and I am getting <u>extremely</u> impatient. "Listen Jésus, I can be your mate and you and I can fish together". Off we went. I drove the boat which was a shining example of Mexican maritime technology. Two unequal size inboard engines and two undersized rudders combined to make the boat an unwieldy and unresponsive pig. Nevertheless, we are fishing 6 lines in a calm rolling sea.

Jésus spots a pair of sailfish coming in for a close look at our squid lure. He tries to entice a strike. They move over to one of the outrigger lines. The fish depart. We notice that virtu-ally no one is catch-ing fish today. As we troll around, Jésus spots another sailfish responding to one of our bait lines. He releases the outrigger clip, counts to ten and sets the hook. Nothing hap-pens. He pays out more line and again tries to set the hook. Nothing. He messes with the line for a full 2 minutes, and

then, in a final act of desperation, he whipsaws the rod vig-orously, cursing and swearing in Spanish. Zzzzzzzzzzzzzzzzz! He's hooked the sailfish! "OK David, tu tienes suerte. Ay caramba!" He passes the rod down to me on the lower deck. I can see the sailfish tailwalking far away in the distance.

Deep-sea fishing involves a challenging combination of skills and i nstinct. On our way back to port, Jésus offers me a job as his new first mate. I reply, a la Ritchie Valens: "Yo no soy marinero, soy capitan, soy capitan!"

Tight lines and Happy New Year for 1999!

Zihuatanejo

Karen and I visited Zihuatanejo several times and I heard about fly fishing for sailfish. It sounded intriguing so I arranged a panga trip with Capitan Santiago of Gitana Sport Fishing.

The set up involves a #12 weight fly rod with a huge fly reel, 600 yards of backing and a floating line with at least a 100 lb leader connected to the fly. The set up also includes 2 teasers – a herring covered by a large squid hootchie, but no hook - one long and one short. Once the sailfish is attracted to the teaser, the speed of the boat is reduced, and the teaser is pulled in using a manual hand crank.

When the sailfish is in position just behind the boat, the captain stops the engine, and the fisherman casts the fly and attempts to entice a strike.

We trolled around for a few hours but didn't see any action. Suddenly a sailfish started chasing one of the teasers. I stood in the stern, primed to cast a large bucktail.

Santiago's timing for stopping the boat was perfect, and I could see a large blue sailfish under the boat. I cast out the bucktail, the fish saw it, then Wham! It hit the bucktail and took off like a locomotive and started to tail walk. Alas, the fish broke off after a few minutes. I didn't view this as problematic since this type of fishing is strictly catch-and-release and I chalked up another "long distance release" for the record.

I have since learned that you can flyfish for marlin and dorado – that is an adventure for another day.

Tulum

We enjoyed Tulum and its white sand beaches and stayed in a small beach-side hotel called Cabañas Tulum which served as our base for visiting Mexico's Yucatan Peninsula.

These were R and R visits, not much fishing and lots of beach time. We visited Mayan ruins and went snorkelling in cenotes (natural sink holes covering much of Yucatan).

My brother-in-law Kevin, an avid hunter and fisherman, showed up in Playa del Carmen on a family vacation at a nearby resort. We found out there was bone fishing to be had in an adjacent lagoon and decided to fish with Ascension Bay Fly Fishing Lodge. The lodge accommodates high end anglers and day trippers, and they had excellent nearly new flyfishing gear for our use.

We headed to the lagoon in a panga: 2 gringos and 2 Mexican guides. Once we reached a spot in the middle of nowhere, they stopped and one of the guides jumped out into 2 feet of water and asked me to follow. Kevin and the other guide then roared off into the distance and we were left at the edge of a hot and buggy mangrove swamp. We arranged to rendezvous a couple of hours later so we could trade places: I would fish from the panga and Kevin would become the swamp rat.

The guide explained the drill. First – safety. The bottom of the lagoon was littered with stingrays that had a nasty spike, and to avoid injury it was necessary to shuffle your feet rather than walk. Second – there were 2 species of crocodiles that were generally docile, but it was recommended not to startle them. I have since learned via YouTube that there are cases of swimmers being attacked by crocodiles in the lagoon.

Bonefish mostly eat shrimp, so we used shrimp flies exclusively. Bonefishing is similar to hunting. You only cast your fly when you see a school of bonefish swimming in a directed fashion. You need a more-or-less perfect cast to attract their attention. The Mexican guides served as scouts to locate the fish and instructed us when to pull the trigger.

I found bonefishing to be extremely frustrating and ended up flogging the water all day without success. Kevin out fished me: following a day on the lagoon he caught a single small bonefish. We could see bonefish schools but couldn't seem to interest them. Perhaps they didn't like gringos? There are more productive bone-fishing areas in the world than Tulum like Cuba, the Bahamas and Florida, but I have already crossed them off my bucket list.

Later during the visit, we hired a guide for a nature tour of Sian Ka'an Biosphere reserve. The boat driver took us to a spot where we could see nos-tril openings and hear the soft breathing of manatees floating just below the surface.

Virgin Islands

I have 3 brothers and in 2013, we arranged a catamaran cruise in the British Virgin Islands and sailed to Virgin Gorda, Anegada, Tortola and the Soggy Dollar Bar – so called due to its dock-free beach which requires a swim to get to the bar.

I brought along a hand line and some lures which I dragged behind the cat but only caught small barracudas.

 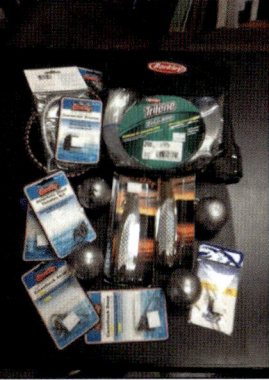 

My brothers and I live in different parts of Canada, so we parted ways in the British Virgin Islands and flew back home. I was routed through St. Johns on the American Virgin Islands where I needed to overnight to connect to Miami the following day. I had time to kill and began to investigate fishing opportunities. Sure enough, there was an outfit that catered to anglers: Double Header Sport Fishing. I called them up and asked about their availability and rates: $1100 for a day trip and $600 for a half day. $600 was a little rich and I asked them if they could pair me up with another angler to share the cost.

By the time I pulled into St. Johns no other charter customers had showed. I weighed up the pros and cons of taking a half day trip by myself and convinced myself that it would be unlikely I would ever return and isn't it true that you only live once? Following this rationalization, I signed up for a half day charter with Captain Tyler departing at 2:00 pm.

The Marina is a 15-minute taxi ride from St. Johns, and I hooked up with a taxi driver named Robert who was brimming with information about St. Johns, fishing, his family and island politics. As we approached the marina, I told him he could have any fish that I caught, and he should meet me at 7:00 pm.

Even within the sheltered marina the wind was gusting and producing white caps close to shore. I anticipated a rough ride. I went down to the dock and met Captain Tyler (ex US Navy) and jumped on board a beautiful looking boat with twin inboards. Before we cast off, Captain Tyler explained that we had 2 basic options: stay close to shore and avoid the brunt of the wind and experience mediocre fishing, or head offshore where we would need to contend with wind, swells and large waves but have a chance at some productive fishing. It was a no brainer – we headed offshore.

We immediately encountered the waves and the swell. Captain Tyler is a superb boat driver, but we still got spray-soaked and spent the entire ride clutching onto the leeward side of the boat console. We stood rather than sat so our legs could function as shock absorbers. Perversely, I enjoyed the ride. We soon lost sight of land and continued offshore as Captain Tyler scanned the horizon looking for seabirds. After 30 minutes-or-so we encountered a huge flock of thousands of seabirds. We set out the lines and trolled through the middle of the flock and right away hooked a skipjack tuna. The fish was only 5-6 pounds but there was huge tension on the fishing line, and it took me forever to

land it. By that time the birds had moved away, and we started trolling blindly, not unlike salmon fishing.

After an hour-or-so we saw another small flock of sea birds and set out 5 lines and simultaneously hooked 4 dorados. These fish are jumpers and to see large dorados jumping simultaneously is quite a thrill. Five lines for two fishers is a bit of a management challenge and there was a lot of adrenaline flowing as we boated a couple of dorados.

I was reeling in dorado number three when Captain Tyler told me to leave the fish in the water behind the boat. He then opened a bait tank filled with small fish ("chum") and scooped them overboard close to the stationary dorado. Within a few minutes several new (unhooked) dorado oriented beside the hooked fish and the captain then brought

out a baited fly rod and tried to entice a strike. Nothing happened but I admired Captain Tyler's creativity.

At that point we had burned 3.5 hours out of a 4-hour charter and the captain decided, "Time to get you a bill fish!". Love the attitude! We trolled back towards the marina and picked up another dorado, before heading back to the marina. The arrangement with Double Header is the angler keeps the first 10 lb. of filets and Double Header keeps the rest to sell commercially. I gave the captain a well-earned tip and walked up the dock with a plastic bag containing 10 pounds of primo, fresh from the sea, dorado filets. Robert the taxi driver was waiting at the top of the ramp and his eyes practically popped out of his head when I gave him the fish. Now that's fishing!

Cabo San Lucas

Cabo San Lucas on the Baja Peninsula arguably has the best deep-sea fishing in Mexico. Much of the tourist economy of Cabo revolves around fishing for marlin, dorado, rooster fish, wahoo and yellowfin tuna. Karen and I discussed a visit to Cabo for deep-sea fishing. Karen showed no interest whatsoever and encouraged me to partner with one of my fishing buddies. However, as the Cabo trip started to crystallize, she flip-flopped and decided to join in provided she didn't have to fish.

I trolled the internet to investigate fishing charters. One of these, Lands End Charters, serves as a broker for 50+ Mexican fishing boats in their fleet and El Torito (Little Bull), caught my attention. I arranged a 2-day charter. El Torito is captained by Antonio Romero who has a reputation as a highliner and one of the best captains in Cabo and I had a good feeling about El Torito.

I walked down to El Torito on Day 1, and we trolled all day. Nada.

As a mature fisherman, I accept that some days you will get skunked. Provided that the gear is presented properly and the captain and crew are trying, I can easily accept getting skunked.

On the second day it was blustery and there wasn't much action for a few hours. We then encountered a stationary pack of boats. A bait ball! We decided to join the fray and successively hooked 2 striped marlins. On our way back to the marina we hooked a third, making for a very successful day of fishing.

We returned the following year, and I shared a charter with a Canadian fisheries biologist, Andy Olsen. Andy is so enamoured with Cabo that he tattooed many of the features of Cabo on his arm including the Arch of Cabo San Lucas, Lover's Beach and the different fish species to be found. We hit paydirt on the fishing grounds: 5 marlins in 6 hours. At that point, Andy and I decided to return to the Marina. Antonio turned the boat towards port, but was somewhat incredulous: why would you abandon such good fishing and run home prematurely? I didn't see the point of stressing more fish, even if it was catch-and-release.

While in Cabo I heard about the Bisbee's Black and Blue (Black Marlin and Blue Marlin) fishing tournament that takes place in October. I asked around about joining a team. This is big-time fishing, and many of the boats are valued in $millions. Some boat owners, mostly Americans, moor their boats in Cabo all year long and are maintained by a Mexican crew in their absence. Some have private jets and spend a few days fishing in the tournament before returning home. It looked like an interesting event. After going down a few blind alleys, I decided to contact Capitan Antonio to ask for his advice about joining a team. It turned out that he was putting an El Torito team together and they could accommodate a warm body to fill their last remaining spot. Antonio didn't know me from a hole in the ground and speaks only basic English, but we developed a rapport that has evolved into a continuing friendship.

The entry fee for Bisbees ranges between $5,000 and $72,500 so having a gringo investor for part of the entry fee was a major plus. Antonio explained that any prize payout (range between $1 – 3 million) would be proportional to your investment in the entry fee, following subtraction of a boat share and a captain and crew share. I have friends in Vancouver who thought this was a scam and I would be squeezed out of any reward dividend.

However, I had a good feeling about Antonio and the other crew members. This turned out to be a non-issue since we were skunked, as were most of the other entrants. Subsequently in the following year, there were no qualifying marlins caught (greater than 300 lb) and tournament entry fees were returned to entrants.

There were 7 Mexicans and one gringo on board and as we trolled around, I inflicted my Spanish on the crew members and got to see Baja California del Sur through a Mexican lens.

Karen and I returned to Cabo the next winter and I contacted Antonio to let him know I was coming. After we checked in to our Airbnb, Antonio called up and asked if I wanted to join a fishing trip he had organized for his family. "Por supuesto. Vamanos!"

We had a good day on the water and Antonio's nephew, 12 years old, caught his first marlin.

I returned to fish in Bisbees again the next year and Antonio obtained access to a larger boat, the *Don Luis* captained by Pépé de la Peña, another highliner fishing captain in Cabo. The boat had lots of amenities including air-conditioning in the main cabin. We again trolled and trolled and trolled and returned to the Marina with little to show for it, save for a great time with new Mexican friends.

While in Cabo, we met Antonio's wife, Betty. Betty and Karen communicated in Spanish and English via Google translation programs on their iPhones and got along well. They asked what our plans were. We were intending to rent a car to visit La Paz and Todos Santos but the car rental agency we booked with was closed tighter than a drum. Antonio said we needed some guides and more ambitious plans to get to know Baja. He had a friend who drove a Honda Civic that we could rent for a reasonable price. Off we went.

Our first stop an hour outside of Cabo was to a dusty little restaurant for breakfast. We were served machaca, which is wind-dried spicy beef served with the usual Mexican accompaniments. We then drove to Loreto and the next day we stopped at a few places including a steel church designed and bult by Gustave Eiffel of Eiffel Tower fame. We then overnighted at Guererro Negro, site of the largest salt mine in the world and toured the mine the next day. Prior to our tour, Antonio received a call from a customer who wanted to go fishing the next day. The distance from Guerrero to Cabo is 920 km so we had a bit of a drive. Antonio and I split the driving, and we drove like bats out of hell, returning to Cabo in the middle of the night. It was a whirlwind tour that we greatly enjoyed, especially the time spent with our gracious hosts. We even learned a new Spanish slang word: "chollero" which means a person from Cabo who is like the spines on a cholla cactus.

Karen and I started a tradition whereby we would do something mean-ingful each year to celebrate our dwindling number of future birthdays. In 2023 we paid a visit to a good friend, Ellen Scanlan, who lives in San Francisco and did some touristy things including a visit to Alcatraz, eating the best Cioppino imaginable and going to a San Francisco 49ers football game. It was a great weekend, and we vowed to keep up the tradition.

When I started scheming for my 72nd birthday in 2024, we decided to visit Cabo. We had planned a visit several years prior just when COVID hit, but Justin Trudeau, our prime minister at the time, warned Canadians that now is not the time to travel on vacation. We respected that and postponed our visit. At the same time a colleague of mine who lives in Nanaimo went to Cabo and unbeknown to her, she had contracted COVID prior to her departure. When she tested positive in Mexico, she needed to wait 10 additional days before being permitted to return to Canada. Cabo is a delightful Mexican town, but restrictions to your movements can sour your vacation experience.

Prior to arranging a visit, I asked Antonio when was the best time for tuna fishing and he identified September, co-incidentally the same month as my birthday. We booked flights and an Airbnb and settled in. The next day Antonio connected with me via Facebook and invited me to join a fishing trip he had organized for several friends. My contribution was to pay for the fuel, a most generous invitation. We used a kite to suspend a flying fish lure that skipped across the surface and enticed yellowfin tuna to bite.

The next day I called Antonio who was evidently out fishing and slow to pick up. I asked whether we could go dorado fishing and he answered with a terse: "Si". I was joined by an American friend, Frank Capo from Chicago, and off we went looking for dorados. Once again, Antonio came through.

Why do I like fishing? It's all about the journey and any catch is a bonus. The best part is going down to the boat in the early morning, smelling the diesel and the salty air, watching the sunrise, and hanging with your fishing buddies.

CRUISIN'

I've always had a thing about boats and being on the water. My family used to cruise on Lake St. Louis adjacent to Montreal where my father owned a somewhat poor excuse for a sailboat called a Silhouette and later, a stunning mahogany Dragon class sailboat.

We also had access to a Flying Junior, a small dinghy used for training frequently sailed by Junior Squadrons. We had some successes and at 11 years old I entered the Canadian Flying Junior Championships which had 110 entrants. My crew for the race was Barry Krumholtz, also 11 years old, and a keen young sailor.

Anyone who has raced sailboats is keenly aware of the importance of the start. As in Formula 1 Gran Prix car racing, the car that takes the pole position frequently wins the race. Our first start was abysmal, and we were at the bottom of the pack, sailing upwind. Tactically, this is the worst place you can find yourself. We decided to take a different approach. The entire fleet was heading towards shore on a starboard tack, anticipating a "lift". We went our own way on a port tack towards the middle of the lake and found better winds (both strength and directionality) offshore.

Dear David, Remember the fleet a mile behind you? Here it is, as it looked to me. Congratulations. Dr. S. Silver

We were the first boat to reach the windward mark by a country mile. What should have been a slam dunk for a win turned into 5th place. The reason for the drop in position was the crew's behavior. We spent most of the rest of the race looking backwards at the 109 boats behind us and didn't focus on the course ahead. Following the race, one of the other skippers told us about "covering", a defensive tactic used primarily upwind, to solidify your position in front of other boats.

By virtue of the Race 1 results and given our young ages, the Racing Committee "created" prizes for us: rigging knives with marlin spikes.

The sailing interest was still alive 25 years later and I began to investigate sailing opportunities in the Caribbean. A good friend, Paul Wolsak, was also keen and, following some research, we settled on the "Yankee Clipper" based out of St. Lucia.

The Yankee Clipper was one of the Tall Ships owned and operated by Windjammer Cruises. She was a steel vessel, 197 feet long, with three masts. The ship was confiscated as a war prize during WW II and used as a submarine scout. She was considered one of the fastest Tall Ships on the West Coast, where she raced off Newport Beach, California. She sailed as a passenger ship in the Caribbean until the company went bankrupt in 2007.

We flew to St. Lucia via Tampa Bay, Florida, so that Paul could visit his Dutch aunt, and then hopped over to St. Lucia.

Travel in 1980 was very different than today and making a hotel booking in St. Lucia was challenging. We settled into a Bed and Breakfast at Mr. Allen's. Mr. Allen lived simply with his wife and seven beautiful children.

We had a glass of rum with Mr. Allen who liked to talk politics and who grew more belligerent about colonialism. He invited us to a neighbor's house for more rum and more political debate. At some point in the evening, Paul and I decided we didn't need to hear any more about colonizers of St. Lucia, so we paid our respects and returned to our room.

Around 06:00 the window opened and there was Mr. Allen. When he opened his mouth, there was a pong of stale rum and he proceeded to apologize profusely in view of the previous night's accusations. He had evidently spent the night on a rum-drinking binge with his neighbor. We took this in stride and had a certain sympathy for St. Lucians, other Caribbean Nations and their relationships with the past.

We boarded the Yankee Clipper at 4:00 pm and settled into our cabins. Passengers were mostly Americans with a few Canadians. There was a lot of excitement, and the polite, prim and proper British Captain explained that we would be sailing at night and spending daytime periods exploring the islands. Bring it on! We eventually visited Martinique, Guadeloupe, St. Vincent, Dominica and Antigua. We were also invited to participate in sailing the boat and "learning the ropes".

Every morning the crew served Bloody Marys and cinnamon buns, a good way to start the day. There was an open bar 24/7 with reggae playing and several new relationships were consummated on board.

We were relaxed when we pulled into a deep-sea dock in Antigua and made plans to explore the island. The Yankee Clipper offered scuba diving and there was a young Dive Master that took divers out to a reef in a glass-bottom boat. I signed up. It was fun to swim out of the shadows and communicate with the above-water passengers in sign language.

Given my previous SCUBA experience derived from Willoughby's Divers Den, I was adept at taking out divers and always followed strict safety protocols. When I witnessed the Dive Master in action, I was astonished by his laissez fair approach. When we returned, I asked if we could go over our dive. He was completely clued out and I wasn't sure whether he had any SCUBA training at all. That is where my questioning stopped but I emphasized the need to get instructor-certified and to consider safety as the number one priority, especially when dealing with foreign guests. I'm not sure whether my mini lecture registered, but I was glad that I delivered it.

That evening we were again reminded that the ship sailed at midnight, there was no head count, and if you weren't on board, don't expect the boat to wait for you.

At around 9 pm Paul had a brainstorm that we needed to find some home-made Antiguan hooch. He rented a motor bike, and wearing only overalls and flip flops, he headed up the road. He asked around to find a suitable vendor and stumbled into a casino and played a few rounds of blackjack. He eventually sourced a couple of bottles and headed back to the Yankee Clipper.

It was 11:30 and I was waiting on the boat. No sign of Paul. A few minutes elapsed and I was getting worried. The prospect of no passport, no cash, and no traveler's cheques was disconcerting, and the crew were starting to loosen the mooring lines. Finally, at 11:45, I saw a pinprick of light speeding jerkily towards the boat. When he arrived, Paul handed off the motorbike to a bystander, passed over the hootch and spilled onto the Yankee Clipper.

I was still basking in the glow of the Yankee Clipper 2 years later and asked Karen if she was interested in sailing the Caribbean. Of course! We initially stayed with Mr. Allen and his family and re-acquainted ourselves with the cockroaches in the bathroom. The cruise was two weeks long and we stayed on board between passenger turnovers between Week 1 and Week 2. There were some local villagers who invited us to a shack for goat stew and reggae. The place was hopping. There was also a tall teenage boy who decided he liked white women. He kept putting moves on Karen that got a little uncomfortable. I intervened and scooped her back to the Yankee Clipper.

Unlike our first Yankee Clipper cruise, the American Captain was more like Captain Bligh, and I couldn't understand how Windjammer Cruises had hired such a cowboy. He would drink while piloting the ship and even his stunning girlfriend from Houston couldn't influence his behavior. One day a group of guests were sitting around a table on the aft deck and a crew member showed up with a huge tray of hot appetizers. The captain decided these were unneeded, so he lifted the tray, pitched the whole lot overboard and then called for another beer. It was a little shocking but there was more to come.

The captain pronounced that we were on the cruise to go sailing and that is what we would do. It was nighttime and he ordered the Fisherman's staysails to be unfurled. The wind was blowing around 25 knots, and the Yankee Clipper started to heel over and crash through the waves. There were lifeboats on davits amidship and when the boat heeled over, they would be forced down into the water, producing rooster tails that projected around 100 feet aft of the stern.

Fisherman's staysails are sails placed between the fore and main masts of a sailing ship. They are mainly used in light to medium air; in strong winds all they do is heel the boat. I concluded that the captain was more interested in frightening the passengers than navigating the vessel: the captain's order did absolutely nothing to move the boat forward, to the contrary, the efficiency of the boat was compromised. It was a wild ride which I perversely enjoyed. However, there were seasick passengers who didn't share my enthusiasm.

A couple of days later we were cruising south of St. Lucia visiting some smaller islands: Petit St. Vincent, Bequia and Canouan. The captain's theatrics and instability made me nervous, and I was giving him a wide berth. I'm not sure what triggered his attitude, but his body language indicated he didn't like me, and I didn't trust him. We disembarked the boat with instructions that we would ship anchor at 2:00 pm sharp.

After a few hours on the beach, we were feeling crispy and decided to return to the Yankee Clipper for a power nap. At 1:30 pm, prior to the appointed departure time, we could hear the anchor being raised and the ship set sail. Several passengers started looking for us, worried that we were still on the beach. Was this situation a mistake or error, or was the captain purposely trying to screw us? I believe the latter was the case.

The combination of sailing and exploring on land kept us busy and entertained. One night Hicks, the Jamaican bartender, offered up some ganja and an explanation of Rastafarian culture. We went up to the bow and settled into the mesh netting, ascending and descending dreamingly as we forged ahead. What a ride!

There is great sailing to be had close to Vancouver and in 1983, we purchased a 24-foot Stoltz Seahawk sailboat for local cruising. We had a budget of $10,000 all-in and found there was nothing half-decent on the market even close to that price point. I went to boat shows, talked to boat salesmen and trolled marinas looking for a suitable vessel. One day I checked out Eagle Harbor Yacht Club and there she was. The boat was in terrible shape and had been sadly neglected for a long time. The floorboards in the cabin were floating, the bottom of the boat was coated with barnacles and mussels and the interior cushions were write-offs. The boat had a sketchy looking 9 HP Volvo outboard and the deck was coated with seagull shit.

"One man's trash is another man's treasure." I thought to myself, this could be the one. I left a note saying that I was interested in buying the boat if it became available for sale.

Within 24 hours the owner, an accountant named Verne, called me to say he had discussed a possible sale with his wife, and they were ready to move. He met us at the boat the following weekend and described its history. He had used it for racing and converted the full keel into a fin keel to get more performance out of the boat. Because he raced, there was a full complement of sails including 3 jibs, a main sail, and a spinnaker. The outboard barely started and would clearly require replacement.

Our deal included access to Eagle Harbour Yacht Club moorage for one month. Given the poor condition of the boat, two friends christened it with the name "Sludge". They even threatened to come back under the cover of darkness to paint this name on both sides of the boat, which fortunately never happened. Still, the name stuck.

What followed over the next month was a Herculean effort to upgrade the boat into something functional. Floorboards were replaced, a friend rewired the electrical system, the cushions were refabricated with marine upholstery and the boat bottom was scraped and repainted with anti-fouling paint. I then purchased a Johnson 9.9 HP long-shaft outboard which provided dependable power for motoring.

The next stage of the process was confronting a question that most boaters in Vancouver share: "Where am I going to moor my boat?" We lucked out during a visit to Granville Island which was just being re-developed. The developer had built a dock, and we were among the first tenants to rent moorage. This arrangement worked well for the better part of a year, but eventually we were asked to vacate.

Previously I had anchored Sludge in Howe Sound and when I retrieved the anchor, it had hooked an abandoned heavy duty anchor setup with a large Danforth anchor, 30 feet of chain and 100 feet of anchor line. I investigated the feasibility of mooring off Jericho Beach by deploying 3 anchors, a large marine swivel, oversized shackles and a heavy dual anchor line to a surface float. I installed the mooring using SCUBA and the system held up well over the next year. I did, however, spend a few restless nights when the wind was howling, dreading the thought of seeing Sludge on the rocks the next morning.

While cruising I would usually troll a fishing line and if we were lucky, we would catch a salmon for dinner. I believe in the first bite theory and began trolling just after dawn while Karen was snugly settled in the V-berth. It could be challenging to land a decent salmon due to the boat's high freeboard. If I had a good fish on, I would yell at Karen to net the fish, "Get up here!" Karen would come flying up, starkers, net the fish and by the time I turned around, she was back in the V-berth with a sleeping bag pulled over her head. However, she didn't complain when we hauled our hibachi onto the beach that night and feasted on fresh salmon and local spot prawns.

Sludge ended her relationship with us at the Heather Civic Marina where she was eventually sold. There is a saying that: "The two happiest days in a boat owners' life are the day you buy the boat, and the day you sell the boat". We enjoyed Sludge immensely and had great times cruising, but it was time to move on. There were bigger fish to fry.

THE ROAD TO THE SQUAMISH ESTUARY

In Montreal, I attended a Junior College and followed a biology track. My interest in all things aquatic led me to enrol in the Marine Biology program at McGill University.

This was not an easy course of study since most of my fellow students were competing to get into McGill Medical School, no easy task. I went along for the ride and begrudgingly memorized the structure of the 20 amino acids and developed a side interest in human genetics. My genetics class was held in a large auditorium and an outspoken student stopped a lecture one day to complain about another student who was smoking in the back row. He stood up righteously and launched a tirade about the health consequences of second-hand smoke, to which the Professor asked: "Does it run in the family?".

As I was completing my final year of undergraduate studies, I began to feel insecure about my career choice. Who in Canada would hire a marine biologist with no experience? Dr. William Legget had taught me about Resource Ecology, and I realized that my interest in all thing's aquatic could be merged with a more practical focus: fisheries management.

By the time I graduated I was psyched about moving to Vancouver and studying at the University of BC. I had been awarded a Post Graduate Scholarship, which, coupled with working as a Teaching Assistant in the Limnology course, provided a basic income.

There was a company in Montreal called "Montreal Driveaway" that would arrange for drivers to take the company's cars and deliver them to other Canadian cities where they would be sold to unsuspecting purchasers who didn't understand the brutality and rust potential of Montreal winters.

Drivers paid for the gas.

I signed a contract and put down a deposit with the company and was asked to deliver a 1973 Triumph TR6 to Vancouver. The TR6 was a fine-looking British sports car, albeit on the heavy side, with a menacing growl of an exhaust note.

I went to pack up my possessions. When I left Montreal, everything I owned fit into a Steamer Trunk and the TR6. I headed West.

The driving was uneventful until Moose Jaw where the rear brakes failed. I phoned Montreal Driveaway, and they authorized a brake repair. I discovered that the car had many failings including a rusting exhaust system and a slipping clutch.

When I arrived in Vancouver, I dropped off the car with a cologne-smelling salesman. His inspection involved driving the car both forward and backwards for 10 feet. He asked me to sign a release and then made out a cheque for the deposit. Following the exchange, I went straight to the bank to deposit the cheque lest the myriad of TR6 flaws be discovered, and the cheque be cancelled.

When I went to the UBC campus for the first time, I learned that the Professor who had accepted me as his student, Dr. Ian Efford, was leaving UBC to take on a government job in Ottawa. To manage this change in status, he strong-armed another UBC Professor, Dr. Don MacPhail, to supervise my M.Sc. Degree. Don stepped up reluctantly, claiming that he had been "Effordized".

This left me with a dilemma. I had little guidance, nor did I have a defined research project. I was clueless about salmon and ended up spending much of the summer of 1975 in the UBC Library.

As an M.Sc. student you typically get loaded down with course work during your first year. My office was in Hut B8 of the Institute of Animal Resource Ecology and the Faculty Members were respected leaders in their fields so just by showing up, you could "learn via osmosis".

I enrolled in a Graduate course on Fisheries Management taught by Dr. Norman Wilimovsky, a crusty and imposing American with a gruff demeanour and whose bark was worse than his bite. He puffed on a large stogie most of the time and would come clomping down the hall with a limp, go through the door of the lecture room and bark, "Open the stern hatch!". The professor preferred cool lecturing conditions and the stern hatch, a door at the back of the room, served to keep the room ventilated. During winter, some students showed up in sweaters and down jackets.

During the inaugural class, the professor outlined a series of term papers, essays, exams and group exercises that we would need to complete. I decided to push back. I put up my hand and asked: "Seeing as we're graduate students, why do we need to be examined all the time? Let's just do the work and we can have a single class grade."

"OK Levy, what grade would you like for attending my class?"

I said," I'm not into marks, why don't you give our class a B grade?"

"So you're telling me that you're a second-class student taking my course?"

From that point onwards, I would hear him clomping down the hall, he would turn the corner and order someone to "Open the stern hatch!" and then ask sarcastically, "Levy, what kind of student are you?" I would then be required to bark back "First Class, Sir". In any event the course was excellent, and we ended up with a solid understanding of fisheries biology.

Professor Wilimovsky's office was a disaster zone with papers and reports stuffed perilously on overflowing bookshelves. Later that year I assisted BioSonics Inc. in Seattle to conduct SONAR training in Lake Washington. One of the participants was a renowned British Fisheries Scientist who had written a book on fish migration, F.R. Harden Jones. He had a sense of humour. We ran SONAR transects across Lake Washington and could see the stadium lights in the distance.

Innocent question: "Why do they keep the lights on at night?"

Harden Jones answer: "To keep the rats from copulating".

Harden Jones was a colleague of Dr. Wilimovsky, and when we said our good-byes, he asked me to convey the following message:

"Harden Jones thinks you're a faggot and an old fart!"

I delivered the message in person, turned on my heel, and walked out.

A DFO Research Scientist based in West Vancouver, Dr. Colin Levings, was undertaking Squamish Estuary research that addressed the fisheries consequences of Port Development. I signed-up not knowing that the word "Squamish" means "Mother of the Winds". My monthly monitoring trips included winter sampling. Following completion of field work, I concluded that only a graduate student would be dumb enough to work in an estuary called "Mother of the Winds".

DFO provided a retired fishing boat, The Active Lass, as a base. She was captained by Sandy Matheson who always had words of encouragement

and a bowl of hot soup waiting for you.

Sandy moored the Active Lass at the Government dock providing a base for fish sampling. We mostly caught staghorn sculpins, juvenile salmon, dog fish, starry flounders and sea-run cutthroat trout. The staghorns were nasty sculpins with sharp barbs around their heads that exacted revenge on fish biologists by slicing into their hands.

I developed an arrangement with fellow graduate students to assist me with sampling that I would reciprocate in future, a win-win. During the sampling sessions we bunked in the Active Lass and headed out at dawn.

One student, Darlene Belford, came up to Squamish to assist with sampling. We roared off from the Active Lass in a Zodiac powered by a 40 hp Mercury with tiller steering. The Squamish Estuary contains numerous partially submerged logs barely visible to boaters. Soon after leaving the government dock, I struck a submerged log and lost control of the tiller which flew out of my hand, causing the Zodiac to turn sharply. I could feel my feet flying up over my head as I backflipped over the edge grabbing a trailing rope and hanging on as the boat spun doughnuts.

Prior to sampling I had discovered an electrical short in the on-off switch and disconnected it knowing that I could choke off the motor if necessary. The challenge came when Darlene couldn't locate the choke, and the boat continued to spin. Darlene eventually choked off the motor and I crawled back into the Zodiac, defeated.

Upon completion of field sampling, I teamed up with Colin Levings to prepare a technical report, my first ever publication.

A Description of the Fish Community of the Squamish River Estuary, British Columbia: Relative Abundance, Seasonal Changes, and Feeding Habits of Salmonids

D. A. Levy and C. D. Levings

Department of Fisheries and the Environment
Fisheries and Marine Service
Resource Services Branch
Pacific Biological Station
Nanaimo, British Columbia V9R 5K6

September 1978

Fisheries & Marine Service
Manuscript Report No. 1475

WESTWATER RESEARCH CENTRE

I worked as a Research Associate for 7 years at Westwater, an interdisciplinary water research centre at UBC. Located on campus, there was ample opportunity to attend seminars and university events. Westwater generously supported me to attend scientific meetings in Alaska, Seattle, Lincoln City, Sacramento, Nanaimo, Parksville and Lyons. The Lincoln City (Oregon) Conference was memorable, and I rubbed shoulders with Dr. Lawrence Mysak, an Oceanographer. I remember Dr. Mysak describing to me in detail the underlying mathematics of the Navier Stokes equations for rotating stratified fluids, tough sledding for a fish biologist.

My Westwater office was across campus from Tom Northcote who resided in Hut B8, an old World War 2 army hut. Tom was an enthusiastic and inspiring Scientist who was seriously overloaded with teaching, supervising graduate students and writing scientific papers. We became good friends and collaborators.

I quickly learned that Tom had a screening mechanism as to whether he could be interrupted. The indicator was the width of his office door opening.

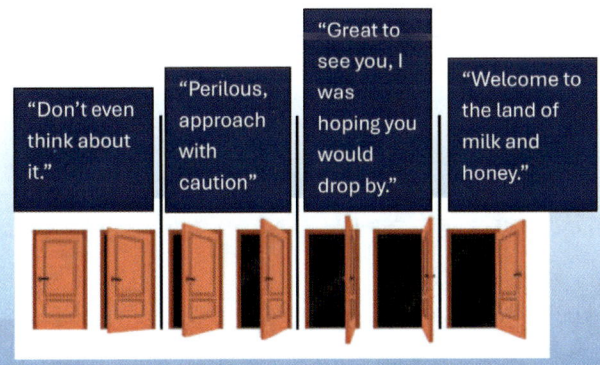

The system was non-negotiable and if the door was only open a crack, better to lay low and come back the following day.

When I worked in the Squamish Estuary I learned about local tides and how they could be harnessed for fish sampling. I applied those methods in the Fraser Estuary with good success. The procedure was simple: secure a tidal trap to stakes at high tide then wait for the tide to ebb for 5 hours then retrieve the net containing a fish sample at low tide.

For the Westwater assignment my instructions were vague: develop a research program for juvenile salmon in the Fraser Estuary. Essentially, I had a blank slate since there was very little scientific work that preceded our investigations.

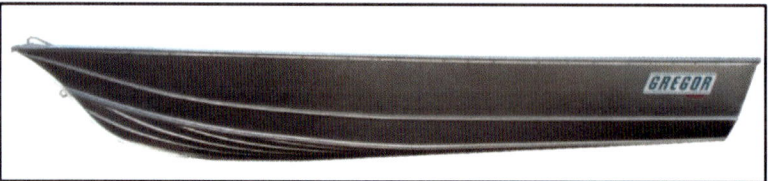

Westwater upgraded our sampling boat to a 15 ft Gregor welded aluminum with a 20 HP Mercury outboard. That little aluminum boat was the best work boat I've ever had the pleasure of piloting.

We also perfected tidal trap sampling by adding removable trap boxes to better understand juvenile salmon behaviour in relation to tidal flows.

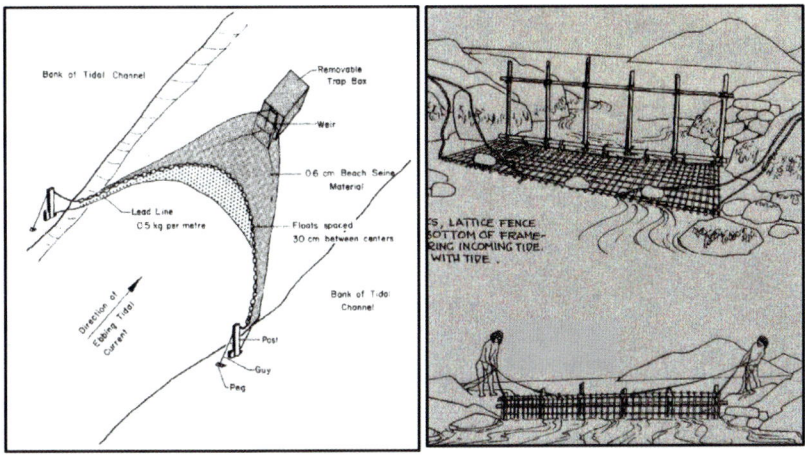

While I may have claimed the method as my own, native tribes for millennia have relied upon similar tidal fence traps that exploited tidal fluctuations to catch fish.

One of the functions of a scientist is to communicate and I gave numerous interviews over the years. During a media training seminar many years later, I learned that you are only 100% responsible for everything that comes out of your mouth. Good advice.

The Vancouver Sun THURS., MAY 14, 1981 ★★★★   GREATER VANCOUV

Fish fry thrive in marsh

By GILLIAN SHAW

The young man in waders scooped an indignant and squiggling salmon fry from the muddy marsh waters of the Fraser River estuary.

"That fry is twice as long and more than twice the weight of when it arrived here," he said.

The man is Dave Levy, a research associate at the University of B.C. Westwater Research Centre, and he has counted and marked hundreds of thousands of young fry that have found the marsh a convenient stopover on their trip to Georgia Strait.

Working with Tom Northcote, a senior fisheries biologist at the research centre, Levy has collected evidence to show fry stop off for two to six weeks in the island marshes. They thrive in the quiet waters.

Levy said he believes the chinook and chum fry are stronger and better able to survive the rigors of Georgia Strait than fry that go directly into the Strait.

"They show a rapid growth rate, there's an overabundance of food," he said. "The salmon that come here in the late winter and early spring survive better."

Levy said the fry are about four centimetres long when they arrive and grow to about seven cm. before they take off again. Their weight goes up to three or four grams from half a gram.

Levy and Northcote have been keeping tabs on the fry, which come from the Harrison spawning grounds, for the past four years. The conditions are favorable: Lots of food and relatively tranquil waters out of the mainstream currents.

About once every 10 days for four months in the spring when salmon start to come down the river, the researchers go out to set nets in the channels of the marsh, which is flooded at high tide. When the tide drops they don waders to collect the thousands of fry going up the channels.

"We've caught as many as 3,500 fry in one eight- or nine-metre net," he said.

They transport the fry in garbage cans back to the research office — a tin shack floating precariously on the water off a private dock. Here the squirming fish — slowed down by a mild anesthetic put in their tanks — are marked by chopping off a tiny section of their tailfins.

Levy sees far-reaching implications to their research, which has been collected in a 117-page report. First, development of the estuary could disturb this natural holding tank which is sending stronger fry out to the fishing grounds.

"The other, implication," Levy said, "is if fish fry survive better (when they leave the marsh), maybe it would be a good opportunity for releasing hatchery fry there." He added that this would have to be carefully planned around the wild stocks.

The research has been financed by grants from the federal fisheries and the Canadian National Sportsman Fund. The fund, which provided $10,000 each year for the past two years, has dried up as a source of money.

Westwater a said the fund for more than organization. has been getti government fo was cut off wit year, he added.

"It's scien Dorcey said. I continue for months, dur try to find m

SPREADING THE NET ... Dave Levy fishes for fry in his research on salm

In 1979 I began to train for the Vancouver Marathon. I weighed 180 lbs and felt great. I occasionally trained with Dr. Carl Walters, a renowned UBC Ecology Professor. I finished the marathon in 3 hours and 26 minutes, not bad for a first timer. Carl was shooting for a sub-three-hour finish and completed at 2:55. This occurred during his smoking days, so he fired up a smoke within minutes of finishing.

Tom Northcote was a highly regarded mentor, and we jointly published Technical Reports and peer-reviewed papers. The paper that received the most attention was based on our Fraser Estuary research.

Juvenile Salmon Residency in a Marsh Area of the Fraser River Estuary

D. A. LEVY AND T. G. NORTHCOTE

Westwater Research Centre, University of British Columbia, 2075 Wesbrook Mall, Vancouver, B.C. V6T 1W5

LEVY, D. A., AND T. G. NORTHCOTE. 1982. Juvenile salmon residency in a marsh area of the Fraser River Estuary. Can. J. Fish. Aquat. Sci. 39: 270–276.

Westwater was contacted by a logging company that wanted to develop an aquatic log transportation system in Babine Lake. They engaged Westwater for a 3-year duration project that would run during ice-free periods. Our base camp was Tukii Lodge at Smithers Landing where we played spirited games of Horseshoes following dinner every night.

Our work documented the disappearance of juvenile salmon from a log storage area in Morrison Arm of Babine Lake due to concentrated bacterial slime that grew on the floating logs. We also assessed historical log storage and dumping sites to determine whether there were residual impacts.

When we assessed the historical sites, we would overnight in rustic cabins on the banks of the Babine River. The Babine is one of the best rainbow trout fly-fishing rivers in BC and is strictly catch-and-release. We would fish after dinner and later sit on the porch swapping fish stories.

We invited Si Simenstad from the U of Washington to sample benthic invertebrates with a pump sampler that he had developed. We overnighted on the Babine River and rented 2 cabins. When I got up in the morning, the other occupants were glum. The previous night, under the cover of darkness, someone poked a rifle into their cabin, demanding liquor, money and fishing rods. Si was packing around a hand-made fly rod and was pretty choked to see it go away. The perpetrator was turned in the next day by a relative and the case went to court the following winter. To add insult to injury, Si was required to return to Smithers the following winter to give evidence at the trial.

While working at Westwater I met the love of my life, Karen, and we moved into a 1-bedroom apartment close to Jericho Beach. Later when our 2 sons Julian and Matthew arrived, we moved into UBC family housing. We have now been married for 44 years and last anniversary I joked that the first 43 years were the hardest. I am exceedingly fortunate to have such a good friend and beautiful wife who has supported me unequivocally over the years.

Several fellow graduate students and I fielded an intramural hockey team called: "The Ecology Animals" and we had a few successes to boast about. During one of the games, I was tripped from behind and went headfirst into the corner, breaking my collar bone and triggering a visit to the Vancouver General Hospital. I can still feel a bony lump on my collar bone today, a reminder of my brief ice hockey career and the need to keep your head up.

One year I hatched an idea for a St. Patrick's Day Party and invited the Ecology Animals and other UBC students. I introduced a game whereby a speaker, wearing a green hat, would have the floor to tell an Irish joke. There were 2 judges, and the first prize was a 40 ouncer of Jamieson Irish Whisky. To kick things off, I put on the green hat for the first Irish joke of the evening. Unfortunately, it fell flat, and no one laughed. I passed over the green hat and the next joke teller had a similar response. OMG, what have I created? Fortunately, the next joke teller came through and subsequent jokes generated huge responses.

The judges determined that there were 2 joke tellers tied in first place who qualified for the final round. First was a polish graduate student, Todd Zdorkovski and the second was Fergus O'Hara, an Irish friend who worked in the UBC Zoology Department. When Fergus put on the green hat and told his joke in an Irish brogue, the crowd exploded in laughter and the festivities began.

Late one evening, during a terrible storm, a man brought his pregnant wife into the maternity ward. The wife was well into labour when the power went out.

While they waited for the generator to kick in, the doctor handed the father-to-be a torch and said, "Hold this up high so I can see what I am doing." Soon, there was a loud cry, and the doctor announced, "It's a boy!"

The man went to put the torch down and cradle his new-born son.

"Whoa there," said the doctor. "You don't want to be in such a rush to put that torch down. I think there's another baby on its way."

The man was surprised. He hadn't been expecting twins, but sure enough — within minutes — the doctor delivered another baby.

"A girl!" he cried.

The man was overwhelmed and went to put the torch down again.

"Hold on a minute," said the doctor. "I think there's another baby on its way." The man stared in disbelief as the doctor delivered his third baby. "Can I put the torch down now, doc?" he asked.

"Not yet. It seems there is another baby coming."

The man scratched his head in bewilderment.

"Doc, do you think the light may be attracting them?"

After our UBC Intramural Team dissolved we fielded a co-ed hockey team we called: "The Rinky Dinks". Our games were casual affairs. Following each game, there was a pub session where we gathered to replay the highlights of the game.

I had spent a major portion of my life at the University of BC. Tom Northcote had me pegged as a future University Professor and suggested that I complete a Post Doctoral Fellow at another University for 2 years so I could qualify for future academic positions at UBC.

I was burned out on academia, we were broke and our family included 2 energetic young boys.

A 2-year post-Doc? Not likely!

SALMON AND THE EXXON VALDEZ

A colleague, Dr. Jim Woodey from the Pacific Salmon Commission (PSC), asked me if I could assist them to prepare three technical reports on Fraser River sockeye salmon. That contract served as a catalyst to incorporate Levy Research Services Ltd. I leased a small but stunning office in West Vancouver in the basement of the Salmon House on the Hill Restaurant and hung out my shingle.

Transitioning to a consultant wasn't difficult provided you kept your financial house in order. I followed a simple business model:

- utilize sub-contractors where possible,
- minimize overhead,
- maximize the number of chargeable days,
- strive for technical excellence,
- remain objective,
- provide results on time and on budget,
- network, and,
- work every day as if your future career depends upon it (it does).

While I was working on the PSC reports, the phone rang one day.

"Hello, I'm calling from Exxon in Houston. I'd like to speak to David Levy".

"That's me, what can I do for you?", I said.

"Did you publish an article with the title: Reciprocal Diel Vertical Migration Behavior in Planktivores and Zooplankton in British Colombia Lakes?"

"Yes".

"I'm calling to let you know that Exxon is very interested in your work."

I was floored. The paper was highly theoretical, and I couldn't think of any possible reason that anyone other than an academic would find it useful.

The Exxon Valdez Oil Spill dumped 11 million gallons of oil into Prince William Sound and is considered the worst environmental disaster in U.S. history. During the spill, the Alaska Department of Fish and Game closed all affected salmon fisheries, resulting in massive sockeye returns to the affected rivers. There was concern that overgrazing by juvenile sockeye the following year induced vertical migrations in the zooplankton, and these became genetically fixed and compromised the productivity of the run.

"Dr. Levy, would you ever consider working as an Expert Witness for Exxon?"

I was cautious about committing and wanted to know more. I told Exxon that I would consider the assignment if the focus was science, not politics or legal matters. He had no problem whatsoever with this requirement and asked if I could meet them in Seattle the following week.

Many friends and colleagues challenged me about going over to the dark side. My approach as a consultant was to prepare objective stand-alone reports that would be the same for any clients whether they be government, industry, First Nations or academia. After working with their lawyers, I concluded they wanted the straight goods and at no time during the assignment was there any attempt to gussy-up my research results.

I remember going to a friend's party when someone asked me: "How can you sell out to the oil industry?" While I'm not an apologist for the oil industry, I replied by asking them "How did you get here tonight?" One of life's ironies.

I have been deeply engaged in climate change impact assessment and mitigation and reporting for the past 10 years and I post climate change articles daily on my LinkedIn site, so if I am biased, it is in favour of drastically reducing and eventually eliminating greenhouse gas emissions. In my view, climate change is the greatest challenge facing humanity.

My concerns, particularly those that relate to salmon, are discussed in articles posted on my website.

Oil spills from ships and the subsequent burning of oil by any means cause environmental damage and contribute huge amounts of greenhouse gases that are released into the atmosphere. That is only the tip of the iceberg and atmospheric CO_2 and temperatures continue to increase.

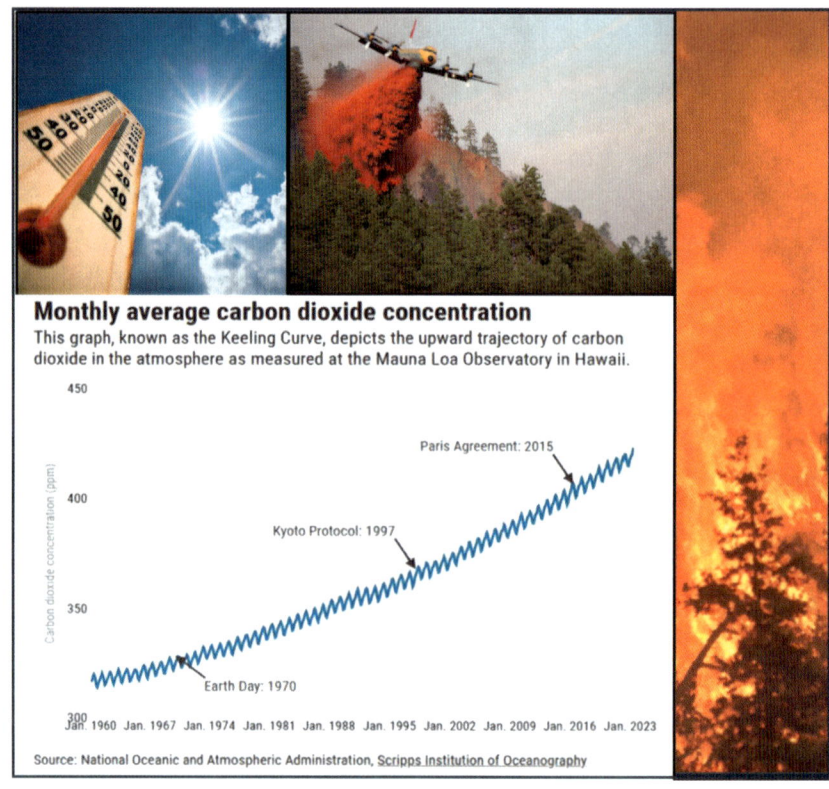

Monthly average carbon dioxide concentration
This graph, known as the Keeling Curve, depicts the upward trajectory of carbon dioxide in the atmosphere as measured at the Mauna Loa Observatory in Hawaii.

Source: National Oceanic and Atmospheric Administration, Scripps Institution of Oceanography

I worked on a team of 6 salmon biologists. The other 5 scientists were American university professors. My Canadian roots came out during a dinner meeting in Seattle in 1992 when, during the final game, the Toronto Blue Jays won the World Series. My colleagues looked glum while I cheered and celebrated the win.

The Professors were smart as whips, and we had lively debates about sockeye salmon biology. The team also interfaced with legal counsel including a sharp lawyer from Los Angeles. He had a knack for asking pointed questions as the discussion unfolded. One day he contacted us to ask whether we could travel to Alaska to examine some sockeye lakes in Upper Cook Inlet. The motivation for a float plane tour was related to questioning during a future trial.

"Are you the David Levy who prepared the report on juvenile sockeye utilization of Lake Tustemena?"

"Yes".

"And are you an expert on juvenile sockeye salmon?"

"Yes"

"Have you ever been to Lake Tustemena?".

"No".

The lawyer chartered a de Havilland DHC-3 Otter on floats, and we spent 5 days flying around the state, touching down on numerous lakes. We also choppered out to "Quayle Beach" to examine residual oil in the intertidal zone. Vice President Dan Quayle visited the beach soon after the spill on his way to brief President Bush, the Alaska Governor and more than a dozen mayors and tribes. When we touched down, we could find trace amounts of oil in the intertidal zone that were visible when you turned the intertidal rocks over, but not much else.

Exxon paid out around $2 billion in cleanup costs and $1.8 billion for habitat restoration and personal damages related to the spill. A subsequent court case decided that the punitive damages awarded to the victims of the Exxon Valdez oil spill be reduced from $2.5 billion to $500 million. At the time, that settlement was far less than Exxon's annual profit level.

As we got closer to trial, the judge who was hearing the case, noting that both the plaintiffs and Exxon each had around 85 witnesses, decided that each side would be allowed 20 witnesses. A shrewd approach and one that removed me from testifying in court.

WHAT GOES UP MUST COME DOWN

Towards the end of my tenure at Westwater I began to reflect on a future that included 2 young boys, a loving wife, unemployment and life barely above the poverty line. I had spent close to 9 years on campus, and understood the lay of the land, the politics at the university and what it takes to be successful.

My motivation to enrol in the UBC Ph.D. program was sparked in part by a conversation with a Peruvian colleague, Salomon Rivera, Head of the Microbiology Department at Universidad Nacional Tecnica del Altiplano. Salomon had completed a M.Sc. degree at an American University and had a burning desire to complete a Ph.D. Sadly he didn't have the resources to pursue his dream, but our conversation led me to conclude that my enrollment in the UBC Ph.D. program would be smooth sailing compared to the challenges that Salomon faced.

I asked my Professor, Tom Northcote, if he would consider supervising me to complete the degree. He gave me some good advice: solve an important scientific question that was testable, and which could be resolved via field or laboratory research.

I developed a research program that investigated the selective advantage and sensory mechanism of vertical migration in 15 BC sockeye lakes. Vertical migration is a behaviour of juvenile sockeye salmon that alternate between resting at depth during daytime periods and ascending to the surface at night. The behaviour is widespread in fish and other aquatic organisms in lakes, estuaries and oceans.

A century ago, Sir Alister Hardy, a famous British Marine Biologist stated: "There are many unsolved problems of pelagic natural history, but one seems more baffling than any other: that of vertical migration."

Just prior to my enrollment in the Ph.D. program, Fisheries and Oceans Canada organized an International Symposium on Sockeye Salmon in 1985 titled:

Sockeye Salmon: Population Biology and Future Management

Around 100 international sockeye scientists attended. I thought to myself "Excellent!" I can present my research proposal as a Literature Review and produce my first journal article. My smugness rapidly disappeared when I saw that the agenda listed me as the very first presenter at the Workshop on a topic I barely understood. I survived.

A thesis committee was struck, and the first order of business was to finalize the research proposal and meet with the Committee to determine which courses were needed to round out my education. The research proposal was already well-developed and required only minor tweaking and I knew all the Committee members. As far as courses, I took a hard line and sold the Committee on the idea that I'd already taken the requisite courses as a M.Sc. student and although some members were disgruntled, they eventually approved the approach.

To prepare for the Qualifying Exam I took stock of my strengths and weaknesses. In terms of content, I understood the science. My greatest weakness was in verbal communication and the ability to convincingly argue my case.

I found a venue that helped me refine my communication skills: Toastmasters. I found that the most useful component of Toastmasters was Table Topics, intended to help participants develop their ability to organize their thoughts quickly and respond to an impromptu question or topic.

- The Toastmaster introduced the Table Topicsmaster, who gave a brief description of the diversity of Table Topics and then called on respondents at random.

- The responses were crafted to express thoughts clearly and succinctly, lasting one to two minutes.

The respondents didn't know the Table Topics in advance and were thus forced to literally *ad lib* coherent answers. Perfect training for a Ph. D. student. When I sat the exam, the examiners were impressed by my newly found ability to get to the point. I felt good about the outcome, but little did I know that the final exam would turn out to be a bloodbath.

I was constrained by lack of SONAR equipment. I arranged to borrow equipment from the Pacific Salmon Commission that maintain a laboratory at Cultus Lake. I reciprocated by serving as a technician to support SONAR surveys in large sockeye lakes including Shuswap and Quesnel. The PSC biologists would then share portions of their data set for my research.

While working at Cultus Lake I was given access to an old shack, "The Cultus Hilton", where I stayed during the weekdays. It was mouse-infested, dusty and noisy but it was dry, located close to the Cultus Lab and free.

Once the green light was on, I conducted my own acoustic surveys in sockeye lakes to better understand juvenile sockeye vertical migrations. Additionally, I collected physical data including light and temperature profiles to test my understanding of the behaviour. BioSonics Inc. in Seattle lent me a 420kHz dual beam echosounder and tape-recording device and the remaining equipment was sourced from UBC. The night prior to the first sampling campaign, I set up the echosounder in my living room for a trial run. I couldn't get it to operate properly and became concerned that I couldn't recover a calibration tone. I faced the prospect of having to resolve the issue in the middle of a lake the following night, while rocking in the boat. I tried again the next morning and successfully got the devices to communicate.

I spent a total of 3 summers driving around the province trailering a 17-foot Boston Whaler from an Econoline Van with a coarsely crafted plywood bed and a single burner butane camping stove that served to boil water nightly for dried soup, a freeze-dried meal package and tea. It wasn't built for comfort and was on the bohemian side but more than adequate for a motivated graduate student.

One time I launched the boat in Morice Lake, part of the Skeena watershed. At around 9:00 pm, the mosquitos attacked and penetrated the van via small cracks in the doors. They were huge pests with a lust for human blood, and I couldn't get rid of them. This induced severe consternation, swearing and swatting. I quickly decided to abandon the horrible mosquito habitat and rapidly retrieved the Boston Whaler and hightailed it out of there. Mosquitoes 1, Dave 0.

The research required that I sample both in the middle of the day as well as in the middle of the night. I didn't have a technician to support my work and chose to work solo in the lakes, both day and night. Today, such flagrant disregard for basic safety practices wouldn't be tolerated, but back in 1985, no one batted an eyelash. I had spent my life around boats, and the Boston Whaler was a heavy-duty unsinkable boat. I was however, very concerned about boat safety while night sampling and while launching the boat.

I had conducted sampling in the Fraser and Skeena River Watersheds, but never in the Nass Watershed. I had a choice of 2 routes: a brand-new highway, Hwy 37, to Meziadin Junction or the Nass River Road. As an Aquatic Scientist I am always interested in checking out aquatic water bodies and decided on the Nass River Road.

I hadn't realized that the Nass River Road was a quagmire. There were no places to turn the boat and trailer around, allowing me to retrace my steps.

I was crawling through the mud at low speed when I suddenly heard "Crack!" followed by "Thunk!" as the trailer became unseated from the van. My first response was to freak out. I concluded that the trailer ball had fallen off and it would be essential to find it. I set up a search grid, donned my chest waders and, and on my hands and knees, I found the trailer ball after 20 minutes of searching and reattached it to the trailer.

I concluded that I had created a cascading series of adverse impacts. Further, I would need to carry an extra trailer ball to mitigate any such events in future. Better yet, it would have been far more effective to avoid the risk entirely by driving down Hwy 37. When the Nass River Road connected with Hwy 37, I breathed a sigh of relief that I had extricated myself from a difficult situation.

To punish me and drill this conclusion into my head, the Nass River salmon gods left me with a goodbye present to contend with, namely, a thick layer of mud that caked the van and boat. I have not returned to the Nass River since the fateful Nass River Road fiasco.

As a young Ph.D. student, you quickly learn that it is much easier to get admitted to UBC than it is to graduate. Your profile at the University matters. Consequently. I volunteered to give lectures and seminars whenever I could. I saw a notice one day about a new course on "Dynamic Programming in Behavioral Ecology" taught by a renowned UBC Mathematics Professor, Dr. Colin Clark. It was non-credit and, following the Professors cheeky approach, wasn't even registered with the Faculty of Graduate Studies. After a few weeks, what started as a class of 20 dwindled to a class of 5. Colin asked if anyone would consider putting their research project forward so that we could work on it together as a class project. I volunteered.

It was a lot of fun, and we undertook dynamic programming and tossed around lots of theories. Colin and I talked every few days and one Sunday evening he called up very excited and asked me to meet him in his office the following day. Subsequently, we published a paper together in a prestigious journal, American Naturalist, which was, and still is, widely cited. The paper was called: *Diel Vertical Migrations by Juvenile Sockeye Salmon and the Antipredation Window.*

COLIN CLARK

18-Jun-1931 - 12-Apr-2024

Sadly, Colin passed away in the summer of 2024; here is the eulogy I prepared for his funeral:

> *"My name is David Levy, and I worked with Colin as a UBC graduate student. I met him by attending his course on Dynamic Programming and Behavioural Ecology. I'd like to provide a few anecdotes for an esteemed professor and friend, Colin Clark.*

My research focused on vertical migrations of sockeye salmon which became a doctoral thesis. Colin was very enthusiastic about working together to solve the puzzle of vertical migration and we began to throw some ideas around. One Sunday night he called me and suggested we meet. We discussed the evidence and realized we had come up with a novel explanation for the behaviour, something that Colin described as a "Eureka" moment.

Colin suggested that we publish a joint paper which we did and last time I checked, it had 690 citations. This is off the charts in the fisheries publication world. While we worked on the paper, I invited Colin and Janet, to come up to Babine Lake to witness vertical migration first hand. We went out on the lake in the middle of the night, and it struck me that this was probably the first time that a Biomathematician had ever engaged in fisheries fieldwork."

As an example of Colin's intellect, we were driving to Smithers Airport, and I pointed out that we still needed an Abstract for the paper. Colin tilted his head back and proceeded to dictate a perfect Abstract while I scrambled to try and capture his words, lest I forget them!

Last summer Janet arranged for me to visit Colin in long-term care, and we had a very enjoyable visit swapping stories and anecdotes. Colin showed me his Fellowship to the Royal Society of London which was inaugurated 338 years prior. Other Fellows include Isaac Newton, Stephen Hawking and Charles Darwin so Colin is in very rarefied company. He also showed me a world map with hundreds of colour-coded pins of his bird sitings, an activity that he pursued throughout his life.

Colin was a mentor par excellence, a great guy with incredible intellect and someone you wanted to hang out with.

Fly away my friend, rest in peace."

Without doubt, Colin was the smartest person I ever met. He was a true academic and would meet with his colleagues, Don Ludwig and Marc Mangel, early in the morning every day to brainstorm the latest insurmountable mathematical problem.

I began to prepare for the final defense. At UBC, there is an examination room and auditorium in the Faculty of Graduate Studies where hundreds of alumni have defended their research. In addition to UBC Faculty, there were 2 external examiners who sent in comments.

Tom Northcote provided some relevant advice. "Your opening 20-minute presentation is the only place you control the examination process. Use it effectively".

I woke up early on the day of the exam, checked out the layout of the examination room and went to the Student Union Building for a double espresso. By the time I returned to the examination room, it was filled with fellow graduate students, faculty and friends.

I gave my 20-minute spiel, and the questioning began. The first examiner was brutal, and I didn't answer the questions well. I was relieved when the second examiner took over, but his questioning turned out to be even more severe. The third examiner was neutral, and things started to turn around with the fourth examiner. The fifth examiner was my supervisor Tom Northcote who threw me a few lob balls that helped to push me through to the end. Following an in-camera session I was invited into the room and given the verdict. I had passed on the condition that I do a few revisions, and 10 days later, the Thesis was in the UBC Library. A harsh end to my UBC tenure!

GETTING HIGH IN PERU

Tom Northcote was contracted by the Food and Agricultural Organization of the United Nations (FAO) to undertake a fisheries assessment of Lake Titicaca in Peru. Upon return to Canada, he learned about a new CIDA (Canadian International Development Agency) initiative: the Institutional Co-operation and Development Program and successfully applied for a 5-yr duration grant to support a project on Lake Titicaca involving a collaboration between the Universidad Nacional Technica del Altiplano (UNTA) and UBC. Tom asked me to oversee the fisheries component and provide support to the UNTA members of the project.

Our team flew to Lima and then to Arequipa for a day to acclimatize to the altitude (Arequipa is 2335 meters above sea level while Puno is 3827 masl). We needed tickets for the night train to Puno and joined a dys-

functional stationary lineup. I could see what was going on: people were cutting into the line close to the ticket booth and those at the end of the line, including ourselves, were spinning our wheels shouting "La cola, la cola!" (The line, the line!).

I lost my patience and walked to the front of the line. I was a head taller than most of the line violators, so I crossed my arms and began to swivel my head through a 180° arc. I adopted the menacing scowl of a bouncer at a popular nightclub and scrutinized potential line cutters who didn't want to mess with a surly gringo. Eventually my colleagues worked their way to the front of the line, and we got our tickets.

We still had a couple of hours to kill and ended up in a seafood restaurant, where yours truly ordered ceviche (I'm an adventurer when it comes to trying local seafood).

In retrospect, dinner selection was a poor choice as no sooner had the train left the station, ceviche revenge reared its ugly head, and I spent much of the night lying in agony and revisiting the marinated fish. To add insult to injury, altitude sickness also kicked in and I was a miserable wreck by the time I arrived in Puno with a splitting headache from soroche (mountain sickness).

Lesson 1: never eat ceviche late in the day as the dish turns into bacterial culture medium. Lesson 2: if you want to eat ceviche, go to a local cevicheria early in the day. Lesson 3: the liquid broth in the bottom of the plate is called "leche del tigre" (tiger's milk, off the charts in terms of spiciness) and should be avoided at all costs even if your Peruvian colleagues are leaning on you to demonstrate your culinary tolerance by drinking the residue.

In Puno we stayed at the Hostal Italia which had a terrace that we converted into a kitchen and dining room. Tom's wife Heather ("Mother Hen") supervised shopping in the market, parboiling of foods to decontaminate them, providing general team support and keeping us healthy.

We conducted a fish sampling program in two areas of Puno Bay: El Agua Negra (Black Water) and El Agua Limpia (Clean Water). There was severe domestic water pollution in the Agua Negra due to the complete absence of sewage facilities; many local people defecated openly adjacent to the Bay. We worked collaboratively with students from UNTA who undertook their thesis work designed to understand the effects of the water pollution on different ecosystem components, including physical, chemical and biological. My wife Karen is a seasoned nurse, and she worked with UNTA to prepare a report on: "Sanitation and Public Health in Puno".

It wasn't all fun and games. During our 5-year presence in Puno, there was a far-left political party and terrorist group called "Sendero Luminoso" (Shining Path) that was active on the Altiplano. The party, led by Abimael Guzman, a former philosophy professor, was responsible for around 25,000 deaths over a 12-year period.

One of the UNTA professors recounted how his neighbour was dragged onto his front lawn, forced to kneel, then shot in the head in front of his family. This was terrorism in the first degree and most of our UNTA colleagues retreated to Arequipa or other safer places in Peru.

Unbeknown to us at the time, the Sendero had an indirect personal impact.

Karen and I were planning to work in Puno in the New Year of 1983. We decided this would be an opportune time to tell our families that we were engaged, and we made the announcement at Karen's family Christmas dinner. Our approach was to announce our engagement then let the news ferment for a month-or-so following which, we would plan our wedding.

The next day news arrived that the Sendero were active in Puno and that we needed to cancel our visit. We put our UNTA work on hold.

At that point relatives expressed their excitement for our upcoming marriage and started to offer advice about venues, invitation lists and travel arrangements for European relatives. Some of the proposed venues included the Royal Vancouver Yacht Club, Cecil Green Park House at the University of BC, the Vancouver Club and Stanley Park Pavilion. Marriage planning took on a life of its own and was heading in a direction that I neither cared for nor wanted. Karen was neutral but also didn't want a large wedding. I made a proposition. "Why don't we get married next week?". Karen's mother took the news in stride and told Karen that "we only have one week for wedding shopping, so we'd better get started." So, on January 4, 1983, we enjoyed a modest wedding at Karen's family home in North Vancouver followed by a dinner and reception for 20 guests at Hy's Steakhouse in Vancouver.

My hockey friends were miffed at not being able to attend our wedding and concocted a surprise ceremony. They took us to the Keg Restaurant in downtown Vancouver. We were led into the Party Room and waiting for us were around 25 friends who were ready to participate in our "wedding ceremony". Karen donned the requisite bridal veil and our good friend Rich Wilson walked into the room and identified himself as The Reverend. He wore a spring-loaded neck collar with an orange plastic caveman that bounced wildly when he spoke.

Thank you, Don and thank you my friends for coming here with me to celebrate the union between a man and a woman.

I am the Reverend Richard Wilson and by the power invested in me by the Peruvian Evangelical School of Marriage and Witchcraft (we curse in divorce), I am here tonight to help unite this couple before us. This couple, of course, Dave "Lumpy"

Levy, lover of beer and fine women, the finest being the lovely Karen. And now....

In keeping with the Peruvian aspect of the ceremony – David and Karen – could you remove your clothes please and lay down on the floor in front of me.

Seriously, my friends, we have come here tonight to just talk about marriage. Now, I know there are probably some in this room among us, detractors of marriage. People that may say that everything smells fishy to Dave these days and that he was caught unprepared, or that Karen, being the professional that she is, could not stand to see a sickness go untreated.

But of course, my friends, this is not the case. What we have here instead is two people coming consciously together, in a state of triumph and trepidation, in a beautiful union that contains more than the sum of them as individuals. But my friends, this union, this coming together is not something to be taken for granted.

Have you, my friends, ever heard of a bird in a cage that would promise not to fly away if the cage door was left open?

Likewise, Dave and Karen, be ever watchful of anything that would cause your marriage cage to be left unopened. For as it says in Deuteronomy 2, verse 6 "Keep your marriage cage clean, my friends."

So hard work is the keystone of marriage – but what to work at my friends?

TOLERANCE – that you will find yourselves safe at anchor as the winds of life shift unexpectedly.

A lovely poem by the late John Diefenbaker illustrates this principle beautifully. It goes:

To keep your marriage brimming,

With love in the loving cup,

Whenever you're wrong admit it,

Whenever you're right, shut up.

I think all the married people here tonight would agree with the wisdom contained in that poem.

So, my friends, hard work and tolerance working at the little things for it says in Isiah 9, verse 5, "Whoever shall not fall by the sword of famine shall fall by pestilence, so why bother shaving?"

But it is just these little things that we must always watch out for, my friends. Well, David and Karen, with this I would end the proselytizing part of this ceremony and say to you, my friends, "If there be any man or woman who objects to this union, speak now or forever hold their peace".

As there are no objections then, with this final act, I would seal this union i.e. handcuffs. I now pronounce you then, David and Karen, united as man and wife. Karen, you may kiss the groom.

Travelling to Puno and thereabouts was sketchy. The area was rife with petty crime, and we needed to always be vigilant. One of the Canadian team members was waiting for a taxi to go to the airport when an attractive Peruvian woman engaged him in conversation. As she walked away, he turned around, and his suitcase had vanished. These guys were pros.

The nearest airport was Juliaca, 40 km from Puno, but the airport didn't function consistently during the

dry season when the ambient air density was too low for airplanes to take off. We used alternatives like bus, train, and taxi.

After several years of quarterly visits to Lake Titicaca, we published a book summarizing our main conclusions and recommendations.

To undertake the fisheries component, we partnered with IMARPE: Instituto del Mar del Peru. This government agency works mostly in the marine environment, but they maintained an office in Puno and a work boat, the IMARPE Uno. I spent a few freezing nights bunking on the IMARPE Uno where some of the crew chewed coca leaves and the rest of us sipped rum for warmth.

While working in Puno, I enjoyed listening to the charango music that surrounded us day and night. I played guitar so I surmised it would be relatively easy to switch to a 10-stringed instrument made from an armadillo shell with weird tuning.

Where to start? Buy a charango. Learn how to play? Find an instructor. That was easy, just go to the market and look for a 3-man group that consisted of a charango player, a zampoña player (a traditional Andean panpipe) and a drummer.

The first group I encountered were very keen on teaching me how to play the charango. My first lesson was 1-hour duration, and I then paid my teachers. To my surprise, they didn't leave and kept on teaching me. Evidently, they had a different relationship with time and money than we North Americans. My teacher returned every few days and prepared charango tabs for me to use and I became reasonably adept for a gringo.

When I returned to Vancouver, I had a mishap with the charango, and it shattered to bits when it fell off my bookcase. A couple of months later I saw a notice that Ernesto Cavour, considered to be the worlds' greatest charango player, was coming to the Vancouver East Cultural Center. We purchased tickets.

During a break, I approached Ernesto and introduced myself, told him about my interest in charango music, and did he have a charango that I could buy from him? Sure enough, he was pleased that a Canadian was interested in playing the charango, and he sold me a bonafide Bolivian armadillo charango. His inscription on the case has faded over the past 35 years and now, with the internet, it is a breeze to tune and play a charango.

El recuerdo para David, con cariño. E Cavour 15/1/89 Vancouver.
A memory for David, with affection. E Cavour 15/1/89 Vancouver.

One weekend, we decided to take a break from work to visit Taquille, an inhabited island in the main part of Lake Titicaca. The lake was unusually calm, and we motored away from Puno under benign, sunny conditions. There was a fleet of home-made wooden boats powered by well-used car engines and they were loaded to the hilt with tourists, the more the merrier. Our party included Tom, Lucio Avila, an UNTA Economics Professor, his girlfriend Gaby, Linda Berg, a UBC student of Tom's and Karen and me. We stayed with some locals in a couple of mud huts that we christened "casas de pulgas" (houses of fleas) for obvious reasons.

When it was time to return to Puno the next day, we hiked down to the small dock that the tourist boats used, and we were surprised that all the boats were still tied up at the dock. There was a strong wind blowing and the boat captains were waiting it out. We sat in our boat and waited. About an hour later the boat captains had a huddle and then returned and pronounced that the wind had abated sufficiently, so we could motor back to Puno.

As soon as we left the shelter that Taquille provided, we were hit by waves and gusty winds. The weather hadn't abated at all, and we changed course to the Llachon Peninsula and pulled into the lee of the shore to wait it out. There were 4 tourists who didn't want anything more to do with Lake Titicaca. They jumped out and said adios and Embarked on a 75 km walk to Puno.

After an hour, the boat captain proclaimed the wind had abated further and that we could now sail for Puno. It turned out that the boat captain was somewhat optimistic in his assessment, and we were still rocking and rolling in a mixed sea state. Suddenly I looked down and there was water around my boots and some of the floorboards were floating. The best remedy for a leaking boat is a pail and a motivated bailer. We bailed out the water and monitored the water level for the rest of the voyage.

Despite Tom's background as an aquatic scientist, he had never learned to swim and while he kept his cool, I could sense his inner turmoil. To add insult to injury, suddenly the engine died. The captain and crew fiddled with it for 5 minutes, then it fired up again. Off we went for 10 min and the engine would die again. We cycled between the engine working at low revs and stopping arbitrarily. Finally, the engine shut off for good.

It was below freezing outside and we all bunched together down below in the dark. Morale started to sink. I asked the captain for the boat anchor which he gave me, and I started kedging from the bow of the boat. Kedging is the action of moving a boat by pulling it toward a set anchor. I heaved the anchor and chain as far as I could, then pulled up the slack in the anchor line. It worked although our speed was slow. I could see the lights of Puno in the distance. As I kedged towards Puno, miraculously the boat engine fired up allowing us to motor back into port. It was 12:30 a.m. when we reached *terra firma* and freezing cold and one passenger jumped out of the boat and kissed the ground.

The next day we learned that 2 of the tourist boats had capsized and several passengers had drowned. This triggered a review of safety pro-cedures by the Puno authorities and limits to the number of passengers. Further, the authorities mandated the use of life jackets, and passen-gers were required to wear retro kapok life jackets like those worn 20 years ago. An official would inspect and monitor compliance, and the boat would then steam off. A couple of hundred meters from shore the passengers would ditch their life jackets which they would put on again just prior to the boat's return to port.

I made a couple of visits to Macchu Picchu when there were few tourists. The first was with Karen and Linda when we stayed at the Machu Pichu Sanctuary Lodge Hotel on top of the ruins and enjoyed Pisco Sours from the terrace. The advantage of staying at the Hotel is you have the ruins to yourself for the morning prior to the arrival of the day trippers. As of 2025, the nightly rate was $US 3000 on Expedia. Ouch! On Day 2, we hiked to the top of Huayna Picchu (the mountain in the top photo) and over the backside to the Templa de la Luna (Temple of the Moon).

On one of my visits to Montreal where my mother lives, she told me that she had one big disappointment in her life, namely, that she never visited Peru and Macchu Picchu. I asked what was holding her back and she said, at age 75, that she was too old. I threw down the gauntlet and said "Bollocks, people in their eighties go to Macchu Picchu every day of the week, vamanos!"

My son Julian joined us, and we flew Vancouver – Toronto – Lima – Cusco where we acclimatized to the altitude and visited the local Inca ruins. We then bussed to Aguas Calientes which served as our base for visiting Macchu Picchu.

During the Peru Project I worked closely with Ken Hall who is a UBC engineering professor. We were working in Puno for a month and were joined by Ann Chapman, a kiwi limnologist from the University of Waikato. Both Ann and Ken were avid bird watchers and wanted to visit the Amazon for a nature tour. I asked if I could tag along. We eventually lined up an ecotour company out of Pucallpa on the banks of the Ucayali River.

Just prior to returning to Lima en route to Pucallpa, Ken got a nasty bug of some kind and he was hurting. We decided to go to Lima as planned and reassess his condition before flying to Pucallpa. Ken's pallor was greenish but under no circumstances would he ever consider baling out of a bird watching visit to the Amazon.

We had some time to kill and decided to visit IMARPE in Callao, just outside of Lima. We strolled down to the waterfront and realized that Callao is the main Peruvian naval base. Most of the fleet was anchored offshore. Ken decided he wanted pictures of seagulls that were perched on some pilings close to shore. He attached his camera to a tripod and fixed a large telephoto lens and started shooting. A small detachment of sailors approached us and seized the camera and tripod. The officer in charge inspected the camera and scrutinized the Russian telephoto lens and concluded we were spies collecting intelligence on the Peruvian Navy. We were guided to a holding facility where we were held for 3 hours. Out of the blue, a sailor came in and gave Ken his camera and telephoto lens and ushered us out the door.

We flew to Pucallpa on the Ucayali River, a tributary of the Amazon, and the town was covered in mud. We walked past the local jail and some of the prisoner's arms poked through the bars while they uttered profanities. It reminded me of a scene from Monty Python, and we quickly exited out of there. We made our way to some small huts that served as our base for the next couple of days while we toured the river and jungle. All of us started oohing and aahing at the bird life in the rain forest.

Among other attributes, the Amazon rainforest is famous for its high biodiversity and productivity. I was interested in the fish population so when we returned from a day of bird watching, we headed down to the local fish market to inspect the catches. On the first visit we saw around 30 fish species. When we returned the next day, there were also around 30 species, but they were different from the previous days catch.

The UBC team got to know each other well and enjoyed each others company. Tom had a reputation as a prankster, and he was usually concocting the next practical joke. I would retaliate, for example, by sliding a shellacked Titicaca water frog, the largest fully aquatic frog in the world, onto his plate while we attended a barbeque. Tom was talking to an UNTA professor and when he turned to look at his plate he wasn't prepared to see an ugly and potentially dangerous alien creature and he flew up in the air, concerned for his safety. Several UNTA profs witnessed the reaction and stifled their laughter lest they offend Don Thomas.

Several months later when we were back on campus, he called up out of the blue and said, "You dirty son of a bitch, expect serious retaliation!" He must have forgotten about the event, because 2 years later he agreed to supervise my Ph.D.

Tom asked whether I'd be interested to present a paper and represent our Peru project at the 22nd International Society of Limnology Congress in Lyon, France in 1983. Absolument! SIL Congresses draw around 500 scientists and provide an opportunity to meet colleagues from around the world. The paper we prepared for the SIL publication was: "A Centre for Limnological Training and Research on Lake Titicaca and the Aquatic Ecosystems of the Peruvian Altiplano", authored by Pedro Morales (the Peruvian Manager of our Project), Tom Northcote and me.

I went ahead of Karen who later joined me at the Congress and took the TGV from Paris to Lyon and watched the countryside fly by. The Dining Car served up canard a l'orange, wine, and decadent pastries with coffee and Grand Marnier.

There were two main social events at the Congress. The first was a field trip for one of the 20-or-so conference tours and the second was the final banquet. Before leaving Canada, I signed up for a wine tour to the town of Beaujeu which is a charming village in the heart of the Beaujolais wine region. Not surprisingly, this tour was the most popular and filled up quickly.

On the day of the tour, we were picked up and driven to the Town of Beaujeu and invited into the cellar of an old stone building. There, we met the mayor who was pouring Beaujolais wine out of a jug, as were several échevin (aldermen). The wine was served cool and had a light taste, not unlike unsweetened Kool Aid. The mayor was very gracious, and she welcomed us before inviting us for lunch at a nearby Chateau. When we disembarked from the bus we were seated at decorated picnic tables and served a French feast. At around 3, the buses collected us, and we returned to the student residences at the Université de Lyon.

Following the Congress, we visited Barcelona and Sitges, an adjacent resort town. Prior to leaving Vancouver, Tom had been talking with a Spanish University Professor about developing a joint research project in the Ebro River delta. The Ebro supported an interesting fish fauna including Wels Catfish, an invasive species, that can live for over fifty years and can grow to epic proportions. The Ebro River is called the catfish capital of Europe. Fish over 200 pounds are regularly hooked and landed by anglers, and fish averaging 80 pounds are common.

I sent a couple of faxes to the Spanish prof and tried to call to let him know our whereabouts. I never did connect with him, so Karen and I were on our own. We took a train to Tortosa, a small town close to the Ebro delta and began to look for accommodation. The day we arrived was smoking hot and we were sweating profusely as we walked from inn to pension to hotel to find none of them vacant. On the advice of a Guardia Civil officer, we walked up a hill to a hotel where we were greeted like royalty. They explained that they only had a single room left, "El Matrimonio", that we would greatly enjoy. Upon inspection, it appeared that the matrimonio had been actively used just prior to our arrival. We had a choice: take it or leave it. We took it.

What next? I figured that at the very least we should check out the Ebro Delta so we asked a taxi driver to take us there. The tide was out but there was an observation tower that I scaled to get a sense of the delta. Following that, we said "adios" to Spain.

INDONESIA: A BIODIVERSITY HOTSPOT

During the 1990's I carried out fisheries assessments in Indonesia, including projects in Kalimantan (formerly called Borneo), Sulawesi, Irian Jaya and Bali.

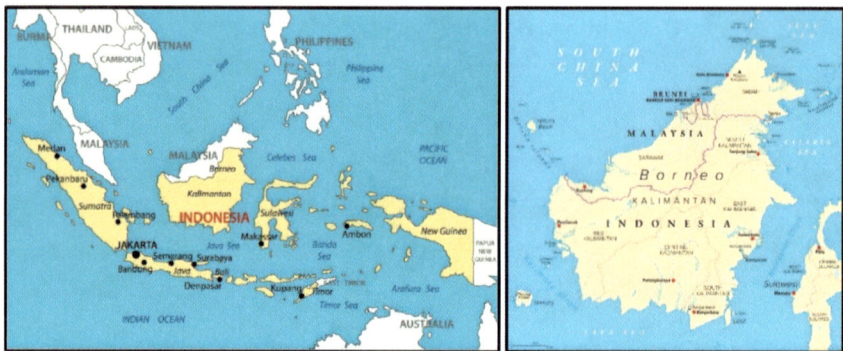

The Kalimantan assessment was undertaken as part of a larger Environmental Impact Assessment (EIA) designed to produce a bankable EIA and a rigorous environmental management program for an Indonesian company, P.T Kiani Kertas, that was developing a pulp mill with a plantation forestry component. The Kiani Kertas pulp mill, was built for $1.3 billion and later remained silent and rusting as financing dried up.

I flew up from Jakarta to the town of Mangkajang, in the district of Berau. We set up a base camp in Tanjung Redeb where we slept, ate and sang Karaoke. The proposed Project was in the Berau River Estuary and required that we boat downstream 40km each morning to undertake field work. It was mostly mangrove habitat that brought back memories of the Fraser marshes.

I worked closely with Ron Jakimchuk, a wildlife biologist from Alberta who addressed impacts on wildlife. The rain forest in this part of Kalimantan is one of the largest untouched and diverse of its kind, with 52 mammalian species (including orangutans), 118 bird species, 18 bat species, 12 amphibian species, several reptiles such as lizards and 45 tree species. A wildlife biologist's dream.

We had a speed boat at our disposal and after a week-or-so of commuting downstream to the Estuary, Ron suggested we spend a day going upstream instead. For two biologists and our Indonesian boat driver, this was a fantastic opportunity to discover East Kalimantan and experience the vibe of the rain forest.

After motoring upstream for around two hours we came to a bend in the river and encountered a Dayak village where we were welcomed and introduced to the villagers. It was initially surprising to us that the only inhabitants were women and girls. The men in the tribe were out in the jungle hunting animals with blow pipe spears and evidently brought their boys along to teach them how to hunt.

We were invited to walk around the village and our Indonesian boat driver served as translator. The girls found us funny and a lot of giggling accompanied us wherever we went. Blow pipe spears used by the Dayak are called "sipet". They are used in both hunting and warfare. They shoot small, poisoned darts with speeds exceeding 180 km/h, and they are accurate up to about 25 meters with a maximum effective range of about 50 meters. The darts are made of hardwood, and the poison is a plant-based, fast-working nerve poison that is dangerous when it comes into the bloodstream but not when ingested, so animals killed this way can still be eaten. Dayak were formerly headhunters, a practice that ended in the late 1800's. During World War 2, the practice was revived during the Japanese occupation of Borneo. It also surged slightly in the late 1960s when the Indonesian government encouraged Dayaks to expel the Chinese from interior Kalimantan.

When it was time to leave, I anticipated a fast ride downstream to Tanjung Redeb but Ron had other ideas. We turned off the motor and slowly drifted downstream. Even after an hour, Ron had no intention of running downstream. We eventually pointed the speed boat downriver and headed back to base camp. The next day we returned to the Estuary to continue our assessments.

My contribution to the project was to generate defensible predictions about the impacts of logging, pulp mill operations and plantation forestry on the aquatic environment in the vicinity of the proposed project. This was a challenging task and required baseline data, an understanding of the taxonomy and behavior of the fish population, developing a methodology for fish sampling and wrapping the results in an effective and understandable report.

Fish sampling in a wide, shallow, dynamic estuary like the Berau River Estuary was not dissimilar from sampling the Fraser River estuary. I dove in.

As we motored around, we encountered fishermen and their families living on float homes and fishing large tidal traps which they set in the late afternoon and emptied early the following morning. They were catching large numbers of juvenile and adult fish and prawns to sell in the Tanjung Redep fish market. I opportunistically cut a deal with the fishermen to sell me their entire daily catch for the next 5 days. They were handsomely rewarded and everyone went home happy.

The traps caught massive numbers of prawns including Indian prawns, banana prawns, giant freshwater prawns and tiger prawns. We would selectively choose a mixture of prawns and fish that the cooks in Tanjung Redep would prepare for our dinner. We ate the tiger prawns (delicious!) and savored the fresh seafood. Later, I met an expert in tiger prawn aquaculture, and he was gob smacked to hear that we ate the tigers. A breeding pair of tiger prawns was worth hundreds of dollars and eating them wasn't a wise dinner choice.

Task #1, fish sampling, was well in hand. I now had to identify and prepare a species list and an inventory of the diverse fish fauna. Fortunately, we had engaged 2 Indonesian experts who assisted us to identify the catch. The most numerous fish present was gulamah, a type of croaker. Within our sampling area, there was a "species flock" of gulamah that were challenging to sort and identify, but after considerable effort we eventually figured them out.

Task #2, fish identification, was largely completed.

Next came the impact predictions which were based on field observations and general literature including considerable relevant information from BC. I was particularly concerned about the use of chlorine in the pulp bleaching process that could contaminate the pulp mill effluent receiving waters with dioxin. The mill established commitments to be Elemental Chlorine Free and would in theory avoid human health risks. However, there was no monitoring of contaminants in the effluent and receiving environment and being a skeptical scientist, I didn't consider Task #3 to be properly assessed.

Kiani Kertas pulp mill

P.T. Kiani Kertas belonged to timber baron Bob Hasan, one of Suharto's cronies. Misuse of state funds for Kiani Kertas was one of the crimes for which Bob Hasan was eventually jailed. Over this period the company amassed huge debts and discovered there wasn't enough raw material to feed the paper mill.

Hasan's aggressive exploitation of forests made him one of the richest men in Indonesia. He was eventually sentenced to six years imprisonment for misappropriating funds from the State Reforestation Program. After an initial house arrest, he served a luxury jail term on Nusakambangan Island from 2001-2004 and was then released prematurely. The Project eventually turned into a financial fiasco and by 2019, Kiani Kertas had liabilities of $330 million.

On another Indonesian province, Irian Jaya, I undertook a 2-week duration assignment on behalf of Freeport – McMoran Corporation which is a global gold mining company with operations around the world. Irian Jaya is adjacent to the Western half of Papua New Guinea and adjacent islands.

Freeport has mining operations in the Irian Jaya highlands on the Ajkwa River which discharges into the Arafura Sea near Merauke; this town served as the base for my assignment.

Freeport's Grasberg mine is one of the world's largest open-pit copper and gold mines. According to mining.com, mining operations and toxic tailings have displaced local communities, damaged food supplies, and destroyed aquatic life closely tied to traditional livelihoods. For 30 years, the mining company dumped millions of tons of mine waste directly into the Ajkwa River system where it flowed into an area of lowland forest. A series of dykes didn't effectively contain the tailings and contaminated an area of lowland and mangrove forest, before flowing into the Arafura Sea.

Why did Freeport want to speak to me?

Freeport contested the fact that the mine tailings

were toxic to aquatic life and hatched an idea to build an aquaculture facility that used the mining effluent water to grow fish thereby demonstrating that the tailings were inert. I prepared recommendations to identify the target fish species to be cultured, local logistics, river hydrology and a plan for implementation. The species selection was easy, and I recommended the use of *Tilapia*. Another important consideration was the installation of a safe-fail water supply system.

There wasn't much action on the weekends, so I arranged to rent a canoe on the coast to visit some offshore islands. My Indonesian counterpart, Melke, was a local fixer who knew how to make things happen. I wasn't overly impressed with the canoe but fortunately the sea was flat calm, allowing us to head offshore.

We pulled up on a beach on a small island and I saw monofilament gill nets in the water and some dead barramundi and dead sharks that were missing their fins. Melke explained what was going on. The fishermen, who were parked on the beach underneath a tarp to escape the blistering heat, would set gillnets to catch barramundi which they left in the gillnets. That night, the smell from the dead, rotting fish would attract sharks that would also become entangled in the nets. The next morning, they would remove the sharks and cut-off their fins which were dried and eventually a broker would transport the dried fins to Hong Kong and other Asian cities to be used in shark fin soup. The most wasteful fishing practice I'd ever witnessed.

We got back to shore after dark and Melke drove me to my modest accommodation. Along the way back, he spied a giant lizard, hit the brakes, whapped the lizard on the head and threw it into the back of his pickup for a feast the next day.

EIA TRAINING IN THAILAND

During the mid-1990's, I worked with various Thai and Canadian counterparts to develop a "Train the Trainer Approach" for conducting environmental assessments in Thailand and SE Asia. The focus was teaching the Thai regulations and procedures for producing high level "Bankable EIAs" which could become the basis for the assessment of large projects.

I worked closely with two Thai colleagues, Dr. Sangsant Panich and Boonruen Pensangthorn. Towards the end of the Project, we became concerned about future sustainability and the persistence of the project after the Canadian funding dried up. We addressed this in part by preparing an EIA Training Manual for Thailand. To produce the manual, the 3 of us met for a week in Koh Samui in the Gulf of Thailand. While I was later accused of organizing a boondoggle in a tropical paradise, we returned to Bangkok with a mostly completed manual.

The second approach was to partner with three Thai Universities involved in environmental assessment: 1. Chulalongkorn University in Bangkok, 2. Prince of Songkhla University in Hat Yai, and 3. Chiang Mai University. I would introduce and lead the workshops and Thai practitioners provided presentations and led discussion groups. The Thai participants were motivated and eager to participate.

During the course of my SE Asian travels I generated a massive number of Aeroplan Points and even reached Air Canada Super Elite status. I began to think about aviation carbon emissions, even prior to the recognition of the global climate crisis. We reward frequent flyers with air miles and provide a positive feedback to fly and emit. It would be more sensible environmentally to make frequent flyers pay more in relation to their total individual carbon loading contributions. In principle, there could be a sliding fee structure but there would need to be a way to level the playing field between airlines.

Karen and our boys joined me in Bangkok for 3 months. My family spent their time going to Buddhist temples, snake farms, canal (khlong) tours, enjoying street noodles, feeding elephants, skating at the World Trade Centre and most of their time in the swimming pool.

Canadian Airlines, my airline of choice, was eventually taken over by Air Canada and operated a route that stopped in Hong Kong (at the now decommissioned Kai Tak Airport) en route to Bangkok. They flew 747's which were configured with business class up front, economy in the rear, and upstairs for first class and the flight deck. On a return trip to Vancouver, we stopped for an hour in Hong Kong and when I reboarded, the Flight Attendant approached me, "Dr. Levy, I'm afraid Business Class is full, would you mind flying First Class?".

"Just this once," I said, and boarded the aircraft. I was immediately given a flute of champagne and a bag of toiletries and received smiles all around.

An agreeable Chinese businessman sat in the seat beside me. When the plane reached 35,000 feet, a Flight Attendant pushed out a cart and offered us a choice of Russian caviar, or lobster, or smoked salmon or all three. Both of us opted for the caviar. They then brought out small ramikens of finely chopped egg whites, chopped egg yolk, purple onion and melba toast. We were about to tuck into the caviar, when the Attendent fished out a bottle of Russian vodka from the freezer and asked if we would like a glass. It was powerful stuff, which we downed while we enjoyed the caviar. Following a refill, we both nodded off and slept well as we headed back to Canada at 35,000 feet.

Prior to around 2000, it was common practice for some airlines to allow visitors up to the flight deck. I determined that if you requested a cockpit visit just prior to sunrise you could see the transition between the remnants of nightime and the initial cutting edge of the sunrise. A spectacular sight and a reminder of how finite Mother Earth is.

UNDERWATER ESCAPADES

I visited Vancouver for the first time in 1975 and was so enamoured by the city and the opportunities it presented that I moved there later that year. I have lived in the Vancouver area for the better part of 50 years.

I landed a summer job as a salesman at "Willoughby's Divers Den". I had no qualifications but was fast-tracked through the diving school and became an Assistant Instructor. Jim Willoughby was an outgoing, gregarious instructor with infectious enthusiasm who loved telling jokes and was passionate about SCUBA. Following pool sessions in downtown Vancouver, we would repair to the "Marble Arch" on Richards Street for a postmortem.

Jim was very keen on finding a facility with a pool that was sufficiently large for teaching SCUBA and the business moved to a new location. Unfortunately, very soon after the move, a student drowned, and the business was shut down. Jim then became Diving Director at the Beach Gardens Resort in Powell River where he continued to follow his passion.

I dove whenever I could on days off and went for night dives after work. Favourite dive spots included Porteau Cove in Howe Sound, Whytecliffe Park and boat dives to the Gulf Islands and Barclay Sound. The underwater seascape blew my mind. My calling was to become a marine

biologist and when I returned to McGill for my final year of undergraduate studies, I switched into the Marine Biology program.

Later, when I was working in Indonesia, I dove in Bali and Lombok. One of the dives in Lombok was memorable and an instructor led 8 divers on a current dive (a boat picked you up at the end of a downstream drift). It was also a shark dive, and I started to think about Richard Dreyfus in "Jaws". The first shark we saw was around 5 feet long, nothing to get excited about. However, the next one was a serious contender, and it taught me the function of fish schooling. We all swam backwards away from the shark trying to position ourselves in the middle of the pack so we wouldn't get picked off by the shark.

The diving in Bali was also an eye opener. The night before our dive, a fisherman had used dynamite to catch reef fish. By the time we dove on

the reef it was littered with dead fish and very little fish life remained. Back at our lodge, we discussed this wasteful practice, and I was surprised by the attitude of the Balinese staff who defended it and pointed out that the root cause for the practice was poverty.

Some years prior to diving in Indonesia, Karen and I visited Israel and drove across the desert from Jerusalem to Eilat on the Red Sea. On our previous night in Jerusalem, we went to a restaurant and Karen ordered a

ham sandwich. Error. Not only is ham non-kosher but her sandwich wasn't fresh. The next day she became violently sick, but we soldiered across the desert the next day anyways. As we approached Eilat, Karen was just hanging on and asked me to find a hotel room as soon as possible. We checked in and I made her drink a bottle of water before she crashed.

I went down to the waterfront and found a dive shop. Could we arrange a SCUBA dive? The Israelis running the store weren't confident about my SCUBA ability and agreed to a dive on the condition that I be accompanied by a diving instructor. As we swam out to the reef, the instructor, an ex-military commando, ripped off my mask to see how I would respond. No problem, clearing a mask underwater was one of the basics that Jim Willoughby had taught me. We resumed our swim and five minutes later he came up behind me and turned off my air. C'mon man, I just want to go for a dive. I took the appropriate action,

buddy breathing. Thereafter he left me alone. The sun was setting, and it was twilight. There were dozens of lionfish with venomous spines that came out of the reef, a sight to behold.

Over the years, I let my SCUBA certification lapse and have switched to snorkelling. We have snorkelled in Tulum, Cozumel and Koh Lanta, all of them a fish biologists' playground.

AMERICAN LEGACY IN VIETNAM

I participated in an environmental assessment of residual environmental effects of the Vietnam War led by Hatfield Consultants Ltd. Most of our focus was on Agent Orange contamination. Agent Orange was a herbicide mixture used by the U.S. military during the Vietnam War. Much of it contained dioxin, an extremely toxic contaminant. The objective of herbicide spraying was to expose the Viet Cong along the Ho Chi Minh Trail, a vital miliary transportation route.

Source: Unknown photographer, 1966. Courtesy of the National Museum of the US Air Force.

Production of Agent Orange ended in the 1970s and is no longer in use. The dioxin contaminant continues to have residual impacts today. Between 1995 and 2004, together with other consultants and Vietnamese physicians, we analysed residual dioxin contamination in the Aluoi Valley in Central Vietnam located on the former Ho Chi Minh Trail. In addition to finding dioxin in soils and pond sediments, samples of human blood and mother's milk had residual traces of dioxin that surpassed Canadian Health Standards. Of great concern to medical doctors is the high frequency of congenital deformities associated with Agent Orange exposure. There is lingering uncertainty about the causal linkage between the spraying of Agent Orange and the frequency of deformities, however, a consensus exists among the Vietnamese that the linkage is real and demands medical support and reparations. Short-term exposure to dioxin can cause darkening of the skin, liver problems and a severe acne-like skin disease called chloracne. Additionally, dioxin is linked to Type 2 diabetes, immune system dysfunction, nerve disorders, muscular dysfunction, hormone disruption and heart disease. Developing fetuses are particularly sensitive to dioxin, which is also linked to miscarriages, spina bifida and other problems with fetal brain and nervous system development.

We attracted plenty of attention when we worked in A'luoi in the Highlands of Central Vietnam. One of my counterparts, Dr. Quynh, was a medical doctor who participated in Vietnam's first attempt to address the health effects of Agent Orange as a member of the 10-80 Committee (so called because it was established in October 1980). Dioxin samples were carefully preserved by Hatfield, then shipped to Canada for analysis.

This pioneering work on dioxins in Central Vietnam led to soil remediation programs in Danang and elsewhere that were funded by the U.S. and other donors.

Soil sampling needed to be undertaken with caution due to the presence of cluster bombs. Many of the "bombies" contained within the

cluster bombs were still alive despite living below the soil surface for several decades.

One day while we were sampling, we heard an explosion close by and found a young farmer prostrate on the ground. He had been using a scythe, an agricultural hand tool, and the tip of the scythe connected with a bombie and blew his hand off. The father was hysterical, and doctors were summoned to bandage the stump. I felt horrible about the accident and its consequences. I pulled out a $100 bill and put some distance between me and the doctors who were hovering around. My Vietnamese counterpart advised me to give the $100 directly to the father so that the cash couldn't be diverted.

While working in Vietnam I enjoyed the Vietnamese cuisine which featured spicy rice dishes, stews, fried fish, barbequed meats and tasty fruits and vegetables. Morning breakfasts included pho noodles in a wonderful broth and sweet Vietnamese coffee.

Our Vietnamese counterparts liked to challenge me to eat Vietnamese delicacies like animal parts for snacks that were chased down with beer. They were constantly testing me by offering exotic Vietnamese delicacies and gauging my reaction to see if I would flinch.

Little did I know that my food habits were about to change.

After I had been in Vietnam for a couple of weeks, Quynh invited me for a road trip with a translator and some of his senior employees. The trip provided an opportunity to talk business. After a couple of hours, Quynh directed the driver to stop the Land Cruiser at a roadside café for lunch. Among other delicacies, he ordered chunks of pig's fallopian tubes.

"This is delicious!" I said. They were duly impressed when I ingested the disgusting meat, washing it down with a Tiger beer.

A few days later, Quynh took me to a dog restaurant in Hanoi. As we were sitting down the sound of a meat cleaver hitting a butcher's block rang out. Barbequed meat was served, and I stared at my plate with dogs yapping in the kitchen.

I ate the dinner and with a stone face said: "Now that was tasty." Quynh responded by inviting me to a cat restaurant the following day. Apparently, there were no types of animals in Vietnam that couldn't be consumed. "Sorry Quynh, I have an appointment with the Ambassador tomorrow". I managed to dodge that bullet.

The next day I was picked up by Quynh and three of his friends. With a mischievous grin, Quynh said: "I am taking you to a very special restaurant tonight!". We drove to the outskirts of Hanoi and stopped at a non-descript wooden shack that had the sign of a cobra outside. I shuddered to think what might be on the menu. Sure enough it was a noisy snake restaurant filled with thick cigarette smoke and the smell of stale beer. My friends pointed out that snakes were a food that would guarantee virility and good health into old age. Diners were eating snake soup, fried snake and barbequed snake. There was a lot of clinking of glasses and loud raucous chatter coming from the predominantly male patrons.

The waiter positioned five glasses of rice whiskey on our table. He brought out two cobras which he released onto the floor where they tried to slither to safety. He grabbed them by their tails and with a flick of his wrists he beat their heads onto the cement floor. He cut their throats with a sharp knife and bled them into the glasses of whisky. He then dissected the still beating hearts and popped them into two glasses and offered them to Quynh and me. My four Vietnamese friends watched me closely. I held up the glass and toasted, "My friends, I wish you prosperity, long life and many children." Karen, a nurse, was dismayed at this gross flaunting of public health.

Unexploded ordinance (UXO) is widespread in Vietnam and neighbouring countries like Laos and Cambodia. While working in Vietnam I met a German deminer - Gerd Willkommen - who is a demining instructor with the German firm Gerbera and works with the Vietnamese government to teach demining techniques to soldiers sequestered to the demining effort.

I ran into Gerd a few times and he invited Karen and I to visit his demining site near Dong Ha City in South Vietnam where he would "save-up" some UXO for me to blow up.

We met the Vietnamese soldiers that Gerd was training in a tent where we shared some tea. The villagers greatly appreciated the assistance of Gerbera and sat on their haunches while we attempted to communicate. One of the values of the demining activity was freeing up agricultural lands that were in short supply. The other was reducing the risk of injury and fatalities.

We arrived at the demining site, and I pretended that I was defending the motherland as I pushed the plunger connected to the pile of UXO. We then drove up the side of a mountain and hiked to the top and were rewarded with a magnificent view of the jungle and incredibly refreshing pools to cool off in.

We returned to the village extremely parched and bought glasses of iced sugar cane juice. We even went for round 2 although Karen reminded us about infectious diseases and hygiene standards. That evening we drove to Danang in a 1970 Ford Econoline Van that required us to sit on the engine compartment beside a vertical front window and pray that we didn't smack into something. Gerd drove like a bat out of hell and navigated people, cows, motorbikes, chickens, bicycles and oxen by waving his arms and gesturing for all objects, living and non-living, to butt out of the way so he could get through.

Following visits to Hue and Danang we made our way to Hanoi and took a side trip to Ha Long Bay.

I was also engaged on another project to provide Coastal Zone Management training and developed both field and classroom sessions for about 20 Vietnamese biologists. This worked well until lunchtime when the more raucous participants would insist that I join them in a café nearby to consume a flat of Tiger Beer. Between the heat and early afternoon beer fuzziness, my afternoon lectures were not as crisp as they could have been.

I asked the Director about visiting the Cham Islands offshore Hoi An and he arranged a visit that included everyone in the office. No one apart from the Director had visited Cham Island previously as access was restricted by the Army.

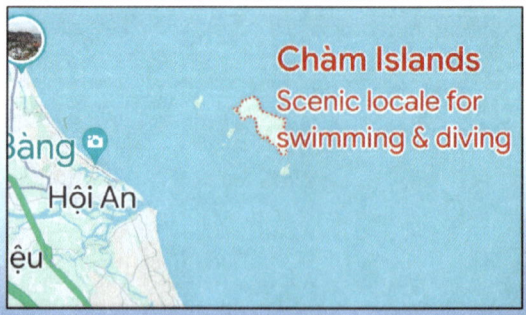

We piled into several canoes that provided 3-4 inches of freeboard and made our way offshore. When it comes to navigating boats, the Vietnamese are fearless and capable of maintaining shallow draught vessels upright. Presently, there is a speedboat that operates between Hoi An and Cham Islands making for easy day trips.

One of the highpoints of my trips to Ho Chi Minh City was visiting the rooftop bar at the Rex Hotel, a famous luxury and business hotel. Its rooftop bar was a well-known hangout for military officials and war correspondents. At its peak in the late 1960s, the Rex had around 600 employees and was frequented regularly by international journalists covering the US war effort. During the Vietnam War, the daily U.S. Army briefings became known as: "The Five O'Clock Follies". This name was struck by journalists who found the optimism of the American officers to be misguided.

When I first visited Hanoi, there were few motorbikes and no cars, and the main transportation mode was bicycle. The bikes were whisper quiet and most women cyclists were wearing white silk Ao Dai dresses and conical hats. Over time, motorbikes crept in and later, cars. The road system in Vietnam wasn't designed for motorized vehicles and today, there is thick traffic congestion, especially in Ho Chi Minh City.

When I was working in Danang, Thai Airways started a daily direct flight from Bangkok, some 30 years ago. At that time, Vietnam had a few rough edges so when I boarded Thai Airways it was always: "Sabai. Sabai" literally: "Comfortable. Comfortable".

GUINEA PIGS FOR LUNCH

Shortly after I established my office in West Vancouver, I received a call from a Quebec-based company called Eduplus, a subsidiary of SNC Lavalin. They were conducting a CIDA (Canadian International Development Agency) program that focused on Watershed Management and Sustainable Development in Colombia and wanted to know whether I had the capacity and interest to co-deliver a training course with an economist from Ontario, Ray Rivers. Por supuesto! The course would take place in Pasto, bordering Ecuador. Pasto is south of Medellin where Pablo Escobar was self-incarcerating at the time of our training course in a luxury personal prison called "El Catedral".

We had a preparatory conference call and agreed to meet-up in Bogota. When the training course started, we introduced ourselves to around 25 mid-career professionals and Ray and I realized that we were grossly unprepared. We innovated. Following the end of a teaching session, we would dine early, go back to the hotel, and then work until the small hours of the night to design the training for the following day. The Brundtland Commission Report: *Our Common Future*, had just been released prior to our visit and we borrowed heavily from the report to substantiate our presentations.

On Day 3, Ray and I had an epiphany: let's engage the participants to prepare a plan for the sustainable development of Colombia. All the participants bought in, and we began to analyze trends, impediments, and strategies to achieve sustainable development. Workshop participants were highly engaged but we eventually ran into a brick wall. None of our strategies and prescriptions were meaningful if the human population was growing. The population of Colombia was around 45 million in the 1990's and growing at a rate of 1.5% per annum.

We then addressed the sensitive question of how to stabilize the population size in a strict Catholic country. Colombian abortion laws are among the most liberal in the Americas and female sterilization is the most common form of birth control. When we broached the question of vasectomy, there was general reluctance by male participants to consider this form of sterilization. Men in Colombia and other Latino countries often have macho attitudes about maintaining virility and the ability to impregnate. While female sterilization was acceptable, there was push back on vasectomy. We could not come up with an acceptable approach to ramp down human population growth, stabilize resource consumption and reduce human-induced environmental impacts in Colombia.

We all worked together long and hard to complete our report. On the final day of the Workshop, there was a TV interview with the governor of Nariño, the Department that has Pasto as its capital. We presented our report to the governor and the Colombian participants vowed to continue the work.

While in Pasto we hung out with the Participants and went on a weekend field trip into the jungle. The drink of choice was aguardiente. Guaro

- the colloquial name for aguardiente - is made from sugarcane and is Colombia's national drink.

In addition to the field trip, the participants arranged a Chiva party (open air bus tour) and we tore around Pasto in a private party with a loud band blaring out Colombian music.

In the south of Colombia, particularly in the Nariño department, guinea pigs (known as "cuy") are a traditional delicacy, roasted and served on special occasions. On our way back to Pasto, we were treated to a lunch of cuy, which was greasy and underwhelming. I took another one for the team.

WISDOM OF THE ELDERS

Over the 20+ years that I worked almost exclusively with BC First Nations, I learned many lessons about indigenous beliefs, connection to the Creator and the spirit world, relationship to the land, political structures, and the strength of family ties. Much of the work I conducted on behalf of First Nations was designed to "level the playing field" to make sure that indigenous interests, including rights, are respected.

An example of an indigenous sharing ethic was provided on an Air Canada flight from Ottawa to Vancouver. I sat down in the window seat and just before the doors closed, an indigenous man sat down in the seat beside me. After we leveled off, I learned that his name was Dempsey Bob, a renowned Tahltan Tlingit carver. He is a member of the Wolf clan and became an Officer of the Order of Canada in 2013 and was awarded the 2021 Governor General's Awards in Visual and Media Arts Achievement Award.

We had a wide-ranging conversation that lasted for much of the flight. When we were half-way across Canada, he stood up and said, "Time to eat", and retrieved a submarine sandwich and pastries. He cut the items in half and offered them to me. I accepted and later thought about the gift. Would I have offered an unknown passenger beside me half of my lunch? Probably not.

Dempsey Bob's work was displayed at the 2022 Audain Exhibition at Whistler, BC, and several of his carvings are on display in the Vancouver Airport.

Many of the First Nations I have worked with self identify as "Salmon People" and salmon are prominent in dances, songs and legends.

During the time I worked as Fisheries Advisor for the St'át'imc Nation, I became friends with numerous St'át'imc and provided advice on the salmon fishery and water flow management in the Bridge Hydroelectric System. I served as a bridge between the Nation and federal and provincial fisheries agencies.

When I first contacted the St'át'imc, a bright and enthusiastic woman, Shannon Squire, asked me to send in my resume which she would distribute. A month later and in the absence of a response, I called her again and she reiterated the Nation's interest in the fisheries assessment. After 2 more months I concluded that the lead was cold, and it was time to move on. Surprisingly, the next day, Shannon called and asked, "Our Chiefs are in Vancouver, can you come down and meet with us downtown?"

I showed up at the meeting and we had a productive conversation about their ongoing negotiations with BC Hydro, and could we meet again in 2 weeks?

When we said goodbye, Grand Chief Saul Terry rode down the elevator with me and we chatted on the sidewalk. I got the impression that our conversation was part of a St'át'imc due diligence process, and that he was checking my compatibility to work for the Nation.

Two weeks later, we met again and developed a work plan and budget. The rest is history. I ended up working for the St'át'imc fulltime for 6 years providing support for their negotiations with BC Hydro that culminated in the St'át'imc Hydro Agreement.

In 2010, I was hired to work as the Science Director for the "Cohen Commission of Inquiry into the Decline of Sockeye Salmon in the Fraser River". The application process was daunting with 57 applicants. At my interview I met Commissioner Bruce Cohen who was flanked by 4 lawyers and other support staff. I had misconceptions about whether the Commissioner would occupy a dais (a low platform for a lectern for the purpose of interviews). Nothing could be further from the truth. Justice Cohen is an extremely likable man and made me feel completely at ease as we talked about sockeye salmon and how to investigate their status. Justice Cohen asked me for my opinion on the crash in Fraser sockeye salmon and I shared my perception that there was "no smoking gun". A similar conclusion was derived by the Inquiry 3 years later following extensive biological and legal analysis.

It was a big job, and I interfaced with around 40 fisheries scientists from academia, the private sector and the North Pacific Marine Science

Organization. Towards the end of the Inquiry, I began to fish around for new assignments.

One of the axioms of consulting is that it is easier to generate work with existing or previous clients, than it is to get new ones. I was attending the Cohen Public Hearings and one of the St'át'imc negotiators, Grand Chief Michael Leech, was present and greeted me warmly. I got to the point: I'm winding down my work at the Inquiry and do the St'át'imc need additional fisheries support?

Every Hydro Reservoir in BC has a Water Use Plan (WUP) and attached to the plan is a series of fisheries and water monitoring projects designed to evaluate the effectiveness of the WUP. When the St'át'imc Hydro Agreement was signed, it included a commitment to blanket award 16 WUP monitoring projects to the St'át'imc. The Grand Chief suggested that I contact the St'át'imc Co-ordinator and to c.c. the letter to him. This eventually led to my appointment as WUP Lead Biologist to oversee the work of a team of consultants. While our work was highly technical in nature, I also focussed on 2 over-riding St'át'imc priorities of job creation, both short-term and long-term, and human resource development.

The St'át'imc and I developed a strong relationship, and I never took it for granted that I had been entrusted to support their interests. When I worked in St'át'imc Territory, I was always mindful that I was a guest in someone else's home. Normally I don't use the prefix "Dr." which I joke as providing the means to get a good restaurant table, however, in St'át'imc Territory I am called "Dr. Dave" to this day which is more of an endearing name than a professional one.

I became Project Analyst for one of the WUP monitoring projects which engaged St'át'imc elders. The project was undertaken to monitor a set of the cultural and spiritual attributes of different flow discharges in the Lower Bridge River. The information was needed to incorporate non-tangible inputs into a future long-term flow decision for the Lower Bridge River.

St'át'imc elders participated as evaluators to score their perceptions of cultural and spiritual values at different water flow discharges. A total of nine variables were evaluated at 10 sites with a scoring system that ranged between 0 (least favorable) and 4 (most favorable). The variable that I considered to be the most informative was "Voice of the River" or how the river spoke to the elder under different flow discharges. We conducted quarterly surveys over a five-year period, generating a rich data set.

There were a few challenges. First, the information was proprietary and ownership rests with the local communities, of which there are 11 in St'át'imc Territory. It isn't possible to show up and expect the communities to fork over their Traditional Knowledge. We needed permission from Chief and Council to carry out the monitoring from the 2 adjacent communities of Xwisten and Tsalalh, which eventually nominated the elders who participated in the research.

Second, when I first presented the scoring procedure to the elders, they looked at me like I was from another planet, and it was critical for them to understand how to collect data.

Third, some of the elders had medical issues, including poor walking ability and pacemakers and it was necessary to adopt rigorous safety procedures including carrying a defibrillator and stretcher in the community bus, holding "tail-gate" meetings prior to the field surveys and regularly updating Safety Plans. Thankfully there were no accidents or medical issues over the duration of the project.

Project guidance and leadership were provided by a colleague, Larry Casper, who was formerly Chief of Tsal'alh. Larry is very personable and systematic, and all the elders knew his family well.

Larry understood how to navigate the politics and administration within the Nation and after numerous in-person briefings, our project received permission to proceed. It was agreed that any Traditional Knowledge information collected under the Project would become the property of Xwisten and Tsal'alh.

The next challenge was technical: how to train the elders to objectively score their perceptions of spiritual and cultural values?

I figured out a way to calibrate data collection during a classroom session prior to the first field trip. During the session, elders scored their preference for 3 different flavors of potato chips - salt and vinegar, barbeque and regular – according to the 0-4 scoring system we had adopted. We went around the room, debated the merits of the 3 different chip varieties, generated scores, and in real time, projected the elder's data into an Excel spreadsheet that generated histogram plots.

The results demonstrated clear preferences for different chip flavors with barbeque rated highest and salt and vinegar lowest. After the exercise, the elders understood exactly how to score their observations, and the exercise reinforced our method for measuring the spiritual and cultural variables.

In addition to field data collection, we wanted to work with the elders to document and collect Traditional Knowledge. We scheduled classroom sessions supported by St'át'imc Technicians with GIS capacity. To kickstart the process I used a computer projector and Google Earth to pull up a satellite image of the Territory and gave each elder a laser pointer to facilitate discussion of the spatial data and their attributes. The group sessions were highly productive and over five years, generated maps with both St'át'imc and English place names. These were complemented by one-on-one interviews and descriptive analyses to describe Traditional Knowledge.

I was impressed, both by the elder's knowledge of the landscape and their understanding of its significance. There was a feature called the "Screaming Rock" on one of the maps and I asked the elders to explain its significance to me. There was some hesitation before an elder described its meaning. In former times when an enemy warrior was captured, he was tied onto the rock and smeared with honey and the bears would finish him off. His screaming would send a strong signal to enemy warriors that a similar fate awaited if they persisted with their attacks.

The Project was both professionally and personally rewarding and I worked as a single shama (a white person) among 10-12 St'át'imc participants. The elders were joyful about being on the land and savoured the field trips and the opportunity to spend time with each other. Those elders that participated in the project assumed special status within their communities.

Based on my experiences with the St'át'imc elders, I concluded that typically, Traditional Knowledge is treated as an "add-on" to the technical analysis, and is often not included in a meaningful way, essentially a "science first" approach. To develop a truly co-operative venture, it is necessary to incorporate Traditional Knowledge during the initial scoping and objective–setting stages for projects. For decades, academics have attempted to "fuse" Traditional Knowledge and scientific knowledge to provide a method for integrating information for planning and decision-making purposes. During this project and previous work conducted on behalf of other Fraser First Nations, I concluded that this approach is flawed and that it is preferable to consider the 2 information sources separately so that one can inform the other and vice versa.

Lastly, the St'át'imc are intimately connected with salmon and call themselves "salmon people". Salmon plays an integral role in St'át'imc songs, dances and legends and historically, 60% of the St'át'imc diet was fish. Dried salmon "tswan", together with salmon oil, historically provided a major component of winter food supplies when other food resources were scarce. Sadly, the salmon runs that migrate through St'át'imc Territory are failing causing a great deal of consternation within the Nation.

ST'AT'IMC ELDERS GALLERY

One of my St'át'imc friends was Chief Perry Redan who would remain silent during most of our meetings, and only towards the end of the meeting, would he stand up and provide his perspective and make a highly relevant series of observations and comments. Perry had an innate wisdom and knew how to cut to the chase.

Perry served as Chief of Sekw'elw'as for much of his life. Despite an absence of higher learning, Perry would sit quietly through

St'át'imc Territory

meetings, eventually speaking out and focussing on the "bottom line". More than once, I was impressed by Perry's wisdom, friendliness and practicality.

I was working in Lillooet one July, and the town was smoking hot – around 35°C. As I drove down the street, I encountered Perry walking down Main Street carrying 2 large buckets of vanilla Ice cream. I pulled over and asked Perry where he was headed. "Headin' home" he said. "In that case you better hop in, so your ice cream doesn't turn to mush".

We had a friendly chat, and he directed me to his house on the edge of town. When we got there, I pulled up and innocently asked: "How long have you lived here?". Perry looked at me incredulously and answered:

"All my life". We said goodbye and as I drove back to Lillooet, I carried out a mental exercise enumerating how many times I had moved in my life compared to Perry.

I have moved many times having lived in London and Dublin as an infant, 4 different residences in Montreal, 5 different residences in Vancouver, 2 different residences on Bowen Island and 2 different residences in North Vancouver. I began to think about Perry's world and his Traditional Territory and my own migrations spanning several continents and 73 years. Perry lived off the land and was intimately connected with everything around him.

EPILOGUE

This memoir takes a broad view of fishing, fisheries science, collaboration and the enjoyment that stems from being out on the water. I am fortunate to have spent quality time with friends chasing fish and conducting research. I have concluded that the main reward from fishing is being with your mates, watching the sunrise, smelling the exhaust fumes and salt sea air and experiencing the excitement of hooking a large fish.

There are several enabling factors that facilitated this narrative. My age and social situation place me in the category of "Baby Boomer". Boomers were born between 1946-1964, a time of economic prosperity and rapid technological progress. Arguably, Boomers like me have had the greatest opportunities materially, educationally, and economically and have enjoyed a good quality of life, but will our grandchildren enjoy similar opportunities? This is an open question in view of the state of the planet.

In closing I wish to acknowledge my wife Karen's positive influence on my life, not to mention engaging in 04:30 starts to go fishing. Thank you for being my amazing wife! For Julian and Matt, keep those lines in the water and be ready to set the hook!